Joan of Arc
and
Germany

Dieu premier servi![1]
– Joan of Arc

LÉON BLOY

Translated By Richard Robinson

---

[1]*Dieu premier servi!*: French for "God served first!"

Sunny Lou Publishing Company
Portland, Oregon, USA
http://www.sunnyloupublishing.com

1st Edition Corrected, 24 December 2021

ISBN: 978-1-955392-06-8

* * *

This translation from French is based on
the *Collection "Les Proses"* edition by
Les Editions Georges Crès et Co., Publishers of
Jeanne d'Arc et l'Allemagne, Paris, 1915.

Contents

Foreword

Sed ut perspiciatis, unde omnis iste natus error sit voluptatem accusantium doloremque laudantium, totam rem aperiam eaque ipsa, quae ab illo inventore veritatis et quasi architecto beatae vitae dicta sunt, explicabo. Nemo enim ipsam voluptatem, quia voluptas sit, aspernatur aut odit aut fugit, sed quia consequuntur magni dolores eos, qui ratione voluptatem sequi nesciunt, neque porro quisquam est, qui dolorem ipsum, quia dolor sit, amet, consectetur, adipisci velit, sed quia non numquam eius modi tempora incidunt, ut labore et dolore magnam aliquam quaerat voluptatem. Ut enim ad minima veniam, quis nostrum exercitationemullam corporis suscipit laboriosam, nisi ut aliquid ex ea commodi consequatur? Quis autem vel eum iure reprehenderit, qui in ea voluptate velit esse, quam nihil molestiae consequatur, vel illum, qui dolorem eum fugiat, quo voluptas nulla pariatur? [33] At vero eos et accusamus et iusto odio dignissimos ducimus, qui blanditiis praesentium voluptatum deleniti atque corrupti, quos dolores et quas molestias excepturi sint, obcaecati cupiditate non provident, similique sunt in culpa, qui officia deserunt mollitia animi, id est laborum et dolorum fuga. Et harum quidem rerum facilis est et expedita distinctio. Nam libero tempore, cum soluta nobis est eligendi optio, cumque nihil impedit, quo minus id, quod maxime placeat, facere possimus, omnis voluptas assumenda est, omnis dolor repellendus. Temporibus autem quibusdam et aut officiis debitis aut rerum necessitatibus saepe eveniet, ut et voluptates repudiandae sint et molestiae non recusandae. Itaque earum rerum hic tenetur a sapiente delectus, ut aut reiciendis voluptatibus maiores alias consequatur aut perferendis doloribus asperiores repellat.

      – Cicero, 45 BC (*de Finibus Bonorum et Malorum*)

Dedication

To Thérèse Brou du Lys

JOAN OF ARC'S GREAT-GRANDNIECE

This book, my dear child, was written for you. It will remind you, every day, that you have the duty to become a saint and – if God requires it – a martyr, in the example of your marvelous Forebear who gave her life to save France.

You have the incomparable honor and privilege of that ascendancy that makes you much more than a princess, by imposing on you the obligation to practice the highest virtue.

God served first! responded Joan of Arc to her accusers. Those three words could have been her motto. Make them yours, my dear Thérèse, and be her heir in that way.

– *LÉON BLOY. February, 1915*

Introduction

July 26, 1914

I

Joan of Arc was born on the night of the Epiphany, January 6, 1412. It is said that, on that night, the cocks in her village crowed with unusual persistence and that the inhabitants experienced an inexplicable feeling of great joy. Other marvels have been recounted, but that crowing of the cocks, that *cantus gallorum,* appeared to possess a prophetic meaning of singular precision.

The cock in the Gospel is, at the same time, the herald of Redemption and of Renunciation. It is difficult not to be seized by that mysterious similitude when one thinks of the infinitely unique vocation of the Maid.[2]

That young, nineteen-year-old woman saves France, the chosen nation, the people of Jesus Christ. She saves France *all on her own*, one might say. Immediately afterwards, she is renounced, condemned, horribly tortured by spiritual leaders trembling with fear for that delivered nation.

Today, nearly five centuries later, one discovers finally that she was a saint and that it is expedient to place her on the altars.[3] But the decree of canonization is delayed for lack of miracles in the course of that life or after that life which was more grandiosely

---

[2]the Maid: The Maid of Orleans, scil., Joan of Arc.

miraculous than has ever been seen. The learned Doctors of the Church continue, and the torture continues
too, in a way.

As for myself, a simple layperson, I ask where
her heart is. After the terrible combustion at the Place
du Vieux-Marché, the stupefaction of the executioner
was extreme when realizing that the martyr's heart
and entrails had not been consumed. The entire body
needed to be reduced to ashes in order to be thrown
into the Seine, thereby fulfilling the formal order of
the English leaders who did not want that her relics
should be collected. Vainly, the miserable executioner
tried to destroy the inexpressibly precious remains by
means of oil, sulfur, and live coals. He had to give up
and throw them into the river, from the top of the
Mathilde bridge, pell-mell with the ashes and calci-
nated bones, under the attentive eyes of the Cardinal
of England's subalterns.

That heart "still full of blood" and that had
never stopped beating perhaps, what became of it?
That heart, the noblest and most generous that the
world has known, where is it? Fire was unable to destroy it. What could the water of the Seine do to it
even after several centuries? Joan, who is still nine-
teen years old at Jesus Christ's right hand, for the five
centuries that she burns in Paradise, – maybe she will
tell us where it can be found, when she is allowed to
speak. But then, what reliquary could contain it, and
what basilica could give it shelter!

---

[3]nearly five centuries later...: Joan of Arc, born in 1412, and
burned at the stake in 1431, was beatified in 1909. She was
canonized in 1920, five years after this work was published.

The astonishment that Joan of Arc gave to all her contemporaries will be nothing compared to the Christian world's astonishment, which has so long ignored her, when the integral Supernaturalness of that prodigious destiny is finally revealed!

II

Of course, I have not been honored with such a mission, but a French Catholic who puts France above everything, and who would give his life for it quite willingly, has the right certainly, if not the duty, to look at that mother in the face and speak to her lovingly.

After Israel, which was called, by distinguished privilege, God's People, there is not one country on earth that he has loved as much as France. Whoever can explain it, let him do so. To say that it is the most beautiful or the most generous of nations – which is, besides, incontestable, – serves nothing, for that divine possession ought to be precisely the apanage of the Preferred. God's predilections cannot be justified except by his good pleasure which is perfectly and adorably inscrutable.

"France," I have said elsewhere, "is so much the first among peoples that all others, whoever they might be, ought to consider themselves honorably served when they are allowed to eat the scraps meant-for its dogs." That is how it is, there is nothing more to be said, and such was, in the fifteenth century, the unique reason for the Maid to be and to appear.

Jesus Christ, sole legitimate monarch and suzerain of all monarchs of mud and ashes, could not have any other earthly realm than that of France. One does not imagine him king of Spain or England, and the last stage of dementia or of ridicule would be, for example, to suppose him reigning over Prussia or Bulgaria. The world is like a vast residence where only a single royal chamber can be found and a single voluptuous couch for the crucified King of France, the other so-called kings being assigned to sleep on the ground, in the dust of antechambers or the filth of stables. It is true that, for a long time, he appeared to have renounced it, the last Valois' stink, the Bourbons principally, having disgusted him; but the House has not stopped belonging to him, and it is not fire that he lacks in order to purify it one day. The burning stake in Rouen has not gone out, and some spark would suffice to set everything on fire. If need be, the crackling stupidity of our Catholics could re-illuminate it, and we have, hard by, a cardinal who would set himself to the task voluntarily.

In Rouen, there was, for the monstruous trial, a bishop, vile among the vile, and droves of theologians and doctors selected with care from among the cowards and the ambitious, in view of obtaining, by whatever means possible, the condemnation of the heroine. Hateful England had need, or believed it had need, of that condemnation of a so-called *sorceress* to invalidate the coronation of Charles VII. It had, above all, the fierce desire to be avenged for having been beaten by a child, and, immediately after the iniquitous sentence, it satisfied itself in the manner of demons, inflicting on its victim the most horrible form of the terrible punishment by fire.

The ordinary stake for unfortunate wretches, male or female, was raised, if anything, just a little above the ground. One was contented to place faggots and wood around the stake to which the condemned person had been bound. Often even, if not almost always, there was the dreadful mercy of *retentum*, which authorized the executioner to strangle the victim before the first flames touched him or her.

The English wanted, for Joan, that atrocious innovation of a massif of masonry and plaster, on the top of which was planted the post, which the executioner went to a lot of effort to bind her to, without being allowed to kill her, difficulty that prolonged the preliminary sufferings of the martyr.

Friar Martin Ladvenu furnished, at the trial of Rehabilitation, the most precise details on that rarely-used mode of combustion and on the cruelty of the English, – she who had seen "the great pity that existed in the kingdom of France" was unable to find any for herself. He affirmed that he heard the executioner say, on the very day of her punishment, that the Maid must have suffered much more than other condemned people suffer, and that was "because of the cruel manner of binding and exhibiting her; for the English had constructed a high scaffold out of plaster, and he could neither properly nor easily expedite or reach her, for which he was quite afflicted, and he had great compassion for her because of the form and cruel manner by which she was made to die."

III

The punishment of Joan of Arc continues, as I have said. It continues by the sottishness and disgusting sentimentality of her Catholic admirers, absolutely incapable of understanding the real mission of that daughter of God. Of course, they denounce the burning at the stake, but the horror they could feel for her is mitigated quite happily by the religiose imagery that consoles them. There is the Maid's executionary stake, like the velour Cross on which Jesus, clearly, would have suffered very little. All comes to pass with extreme gentleness, and nothing is easier for comfortable devotees than to follow, in automobiles, their Redeemer crowned with thorns. I have been shown a small Joan of Arc in fake bronze on her knees, in her armor, on a padded prie-Dieu taking after Saint Clotilde or Saint Thomas Aquinas. So-called Christian art demands those profanations and those idiocies. The extremity of Suffering has become as inconceivable as the plenitude of the Faith, and the worldly clergy do not approve of the excessive *configuration* of Martyrs.

What could today's populace understand about piety from Joan of Arc, their being a thousand times inferior to those poor folk then who sobbed as they watched the Saint of France dying? In the fifteenth century, they understood at least that an extraordinary thing was happening, that someone come from God was expiring for them, in terrible torments, and that there was no means to be consoled.

Ah! clearly, in those distant days, they did not know exactly what it meant, the word "fatherland," which word, moreover, barely existed. The feudal regime, fallen from its original grandeur, had so divided the earth; and each tree trunk, in a manner of speaking, was so continually claimed by foreign competitors that something like a revelation was needed for France to become conscious of itself. Joan of Arc specifically had brought that revelation, from her Barrois and from her Lorraine, revelation that was going to change the face of the world. Unable to understand, the humble folk, always crushed underfoot by the warriors, felt it in a vague way. Then, Joan was a marvelous virgin, and Jesus, true King of France, bled before her on his Cross.

She had seen the excessive misery of Charles VII, son of Isabeau,[4] who so hatefully had to abandon her,[5] and it is because of him, doubtless, that she spoke of "the great pity that was in the French realm."

Everyone knows that at no other epoch was France so close to perishing. Nine years before the apparition of the Maid, the Treaty of Troyes had been or appeared to have been the unremitting blow. The hateful German Isabeau, abusing her spouse's dementia, had disinherited and renounced the dauphin Charles, her son, to the benefit of that English pirate Henry V, thus become King of France and England.

That extreme shame, it is true, had not been accepted. Around the inert heir of Philippe-Auguste and Saint Louis, there were still some redoubtable combatants like Saintrailles and above all La Hire, the

---

[4]Isabeau: Isabeau of Bavaria, 1370-1435, mother of Charles VII.

[5]her: Joan of Arc.

Ajax of desperate battles; but since the disaster of Verneul, one could well believe that there was no longer any benediction. Charles VII without an army, without money, and without courage, doubting even, as the son of a prostitute, his own royal extraction, was already thinking of retiring to Spain or Scotland to live as a dispossessed prince...

The things of this world being infallibly arranged, it is impossible and unreasonable to conjecture about history. To imagine what could have happened without the Maid is as perfectly pointless as to suppose a battle of Waterloo that had not been lost. There is not, in all of history, as evident a predestination as that of Joan of Arc's, and therefore the miraculous vocation of France is found to be indisputably corroborated.

It was a question then of the realm, of the realm alone, and it was quite nearly an instauration. Charles VII's more or less great predecessors, Saint Louis included, had been kings of France, but not of "all France," as Joan understood it, and it was given to that little runt to make a start of it. Starting with him, the magnificent tree did not stop growing until perfect unity of the incomparable Nation was realized. With that result obtained, the dynastic and *fictive* royalty, which had been the means, naturally had to end like an old oak tree run out of sap, split by lightning, mutilated by storms, gnawed on by beasts, and producing nothing but vigorless shoots anymore.

IV

Integral, homogenous France, geographic France, such as one knows it for three hundred years now, was necessary to God because, without France, he would not have been and would not be, completely, God. Whatever its infidelities or crimes, however terrifying might be the expiation, he will not permit France to succumb, having need of France for his proper Glory, and the fetid Lutherans who mutilate it, for nearly half a century now, will be flagellated with unimaginable rigor.

The filthiest people on earth dared to lay a hand on Joan of Arc's fatherland even, on Lorraine, and it is one of the most overwhelming proofs of divine patience that they have not yet been castigated for that attack. The beautiful virgin of Domremy had, doubtless, foreknowledge of those and many other things, because so extraordinary a Mission as hers cannot appear separable from prophetic divination.

One reads in the astonishing life of the Curé d'Ars[6] that, at the time of his infancy, the mendicant Saint Benedict Labre received hospitality at the house of his father and that as he was leaving he left a marvelous benediction. One can believe that something similar must have happened in Chinon between Joan of Arc and Louis XI who certainly did not become a saint, but who had to be, by divine decree, the builder of the French monarchy.

He was six years old then, and Joan of Arc

---

[6]Curé d'Ars: Saint Jean Vianney, 1786-1859. His grandparents are reported to have given Saint Joseph Labre hospitality.

must have regarded that child with a very particular attention. She must have fixed on him those same eyes that had contemplated Saint Michael and the Auxiliary Saints. A patch of expanse of the blue of France, which divinely enveloped the predestined saint, clearly fell on that little creature, innocent still and sleeping behind curtains of lightning...

What Charles VII's successor was exactly is not easy to say, even today. It is even harder when one does not understand at all anymore what monarchy by divine right meant five centuries ago, nor the mysterious force of that sublime prejudice. Louis XI's enemies, the domestics of nobility cut down by him, wanted passionately to make him out to be a parricide, a fratricide, a perfidious tyrant, a hypocrite, an executioner. Modern historians want it as well, and his legend is powerfully accredited.

But it was given to that great man the task of perfecting Joan's work, which was not only to chase the English "out of France completely," but to realize truly the Kingdom of Jesus Christ, the *Lieutenancy*, as she called it, one France, united and compact, from the Pyrenees to Flanders, and from the Ocean to the Alps and to the Rhine.

The divine story of that realm is like a Breviary whose *Matins* have three nocturns: the Merovingians, time of episcopal hives and Christianization of the barbarous world; the Carolingians, time of rigorous cellules of Feudalism for the formation of that iron chivalry that waged the Crusades; the Capetians before coming, after four hundred years of sin, with intermittent heroism and infinite grief, to the formida-

ble *Miserere* of Louis XI whom Joan of Arc desig-
nates in order to chant in her manner *Lauds* of the
Monarchy, while amalgamating forever the races and
provinces piled up under its terrible press. Finally,
four new centuries having flowed since then, it is the
immense Canticle of the Children of France in Napoleon's furnace. Today we are at the little Hours,
while waiting for Vespers, which will be what God
wanted... the *Great Evening* perhaps.

In summary: From Clovis to Charlemagne, a
barbarous chaos at the stable's threshold where the
Son of God's Church was born, and nothing; from
Charlemagne to Hugh Capet, the feudal framework
with the lugubrious chant of litanies by the same
Church invoking Christ and all his saints against the
fury of the unleashed Normand pagans, and nothing
more; from Hugh Capet to Louis XI, enraged
famines, the conquest of England, the Crusades, the
Interdiction of Philippe-Auguste, the prayer of Saint
Louis, the Thirteenth Century's enormous grandeur,
the black plague, the Hundred Years War, and the
Maid to finish things up; from Louis XI to Napoleon,
the ignominy of the last Valois, the inexpressible
stink of the Bourbons, and the Guillotine. But Joan of
Arc's place is unprecedented.

V

Without her, nothing is possible, before and after,
given everything depends on her. She is the keystone.

"A woman has lost the kingdom, a girl will

save it," she said, before quitting her village. The woman, evidently, was Isabeau, the bitch of the Treaty of Troyes, and the girl, it was she. But infinitely above and beyond the words and their immediate application, there is their interior and prophetic meaning. "What Eve lost, Mary will save." The epoch was still one of mysticism, and it is something like that that her contemporaries must have understood her. The words of that little visionary of Domremy assuredly exceeded her own thought. The "woman," doubtless, could be commonly supposed to be France in the two or three horrible centuries that had gone before, and the France to come could have also been announced and prefigured by the Virgin of Domremy. Ah! it was really something else altogether!

In the deepest mystical sense, the *real* woman, the only woman, necessarily, is the Virgin, and her perfect Virginity is the tabernacle of the Holy Spirit. The abominably profaned kingdom of the Son of God could not, in the fifteenth century, be saved except by a virgin. To speak precisely, to tell all, a virgin was needed to give birth to it, for that kingdom existed at that time in divine Thought only.

The Vocation of the Maid appeared then like the prodigy of the centuries, the greatest miracle since the Incarnation. That, by virtue of the infinite preeminence of the new people of Christian promise.

The first woman to come along is already a total mystery, as one cannot find better than earthly Paradise to symbolize her. So well does she centralize all human covetousness and concupiscence! But the Virgin is the object of divine concupiscence, and the

Holy Spirit, which is Love itself, does not resist her. She can engender by Him then, and that is the whole story of the mysterious Joan of Arc giving to God a kingdom that did not visibly exist before and that, without her, would have been unable to be born.

From the beginning, everything is promised to Woman, and it is by Woman that all must be fulfilled. Between her and the Holy Spirit there is such an affinity that one can humanly confound them, and it is difficult not to imagine, along with certain Mystics, a Third Kingdom, that is to say the triumph of the Paraclete, procured by Her about whom it is said that she "will laugh on the Last Day."

It is dangerous and scarcely licit for Christians to pause at such a thought which belongs to the domain reserved to God, the key to which he confides to nobody. That said, when one is on one's knees and completely in tears, when one is panting with desire and the burning heart no longer knows where to go, – how not to see or understand the Immaculate Virgin who weeps over there, on that mountain of the Dauphiné,[7] and who speaks to her people like the celestial Father might speak? How not to feel, at such a moment, the enormity of the Mystery and the sublime presumption of some supernatural peripeteia that is beyond human understanding, where Woman par excellence, the distinguished Vase, would manifest itself finally in unimaginable glory, in order to fulfill everything?

---

[7]who weeps over there...: La Salette. See *She Who Weeps*, Bloy. In English translation by Sunny Lou Publishing, 2021.

VI

Joan of Arc is the very palpable prefiguration of that woman victorious over men and demons, and there is nothing more specific in any history. Her contemporaries guessed at it vaguely. Quite often she needed all her candor of a shepherdess of Paradise and all the strength of her invincible faith to resist the extraordinary enthusiasm of simple souls who saw in her an emanation of Divinity.

Filled with the Holy Spirit, as her life and above all her death demonstrated, absolutely alone in the midst of crowds, she was allied with *Fire*, visible and redoubtable symbol of Love, in the same way that, later, Napoleon was affiliated with Thunder, and it is a feast for thought to forget, for one instant, the intermediary centuries, while drawing both one and the other of those two incomparable destinies close to each other: Joan believing in the very particular kingdom of Jesus Christ, and Napoleon dilating prodigiously that kingdom in order to erect the grandiose image of the future Empire of the Holy Spirit!

But who can have such a vision? History thus regarded resembles a gulf, immense as all spaces, where the whirlpools of darkness alternate continually with the whirlpools of Light for the blinding of the frightened spectator.

However impassive one might be, one envies, at such moments, the simplicity of all the little ones to whom Jesus declares that those things, so deeply hidden to sages and wisemen, will be revealed one day by his Father who is in heaven.

Preliminary Meditation

November 5. – After three months, I can finally take up again this book which was brutally interrupted by the German war, an unjust and cruel war, if ever there was one, a war of races, as in the fifteenth century, but with an apocalyptic exorbitance.[8]

At the time of Joan of Arc, the strongest armies, English or French, did not exceed twenty thousand combatants, and the fate of an empire was decided in several hours. Today, millions of soldiers are affronted on immense plains, battles last for weeks, and rivers, filled with cadavers, overflow their banks. Already, the population of twenty great cities would not equal the total number of dead after three months. The Mercenary War,[9] more than two thousand years ago, was said to be *inexpiable*. What term should be given to this one? It is not a matter even of conquests, it is extermination that is ordered, total and irreparable extermination of men and things.

From day one, it was necessary that either France no longer exist or the German Empire be annihilated. No possible compromise. Hatreds on both sides have exceeded all measure, and Europe, fearing

---

[8]After three months...: see *On the Threshold of the Apocalypse*, Bloy's last journal, in which he discusses, among other things, various moments in the life of writing *Joan of Arc and Germany*.

[9]Mercenary War: possibly a reference to the war (241-238 BC) between north African settlements and the Carthaginians, on Carthaginian soil, which started right after the First Punic War with Rome had ended.

to see all its sources dry up, intervenes with a fury. The monstrous German expansion is combatted at the same time by France, Russia, England. Twelve or fifteen million images of the living God destroying each other in the crepuscule of all civilization, from occident to extreme orient! Vision of Patmos! Could an angel even say when it will end?

Joan of Arc's Lorraine was, since 1870, under the feet of brutes, intolerable profanation before God and men. Where is she now, the sacred girl? What has become of her after 483 years? She was dying then cruelly for having delivered France from the English. Would she hear the Voices today to chase the Germans out of our Godless Republic? And what Voices? The Virgin of virgins, Herself, was unable to get anyone to listen to her! She wept, however, the Sorrowful One, and her people, Hers, they were all the people signified by the one France. Joan of Arc had caught a glimpse of it in the prophetic half light, without any other immediate apperception than the poor kingdom of her time and the "great pity that was in that kingdom." For her that was everything, and no more was needed in the fifteenth century in order to accomplish the most astonishing miracle in History.

It is indispensable to recall that that old century was Christian; no longer, it is true, the Christianity of the Catacombs or the Arenas, but of dark misery and infinite sadness. From the religious enthusiasm that had made the Crusades there was still enough faith however to consider Christ's Wounds, and, from there, it was able to carry the wine of Hope that germinates fecund virgins.

Now what remains, if not, as Isaiah says, "two or three olives at the end of a branch, at most four or five at the crown of the tree, after it was strongly shaken"? With that, the alliance with Protestant England that had Joan of Arc burned prior to assassinating Napoleon, and the alliance with schismatic Russia that the Visionary of Dulmen[10] saw, one hundred years ago, like an immense country enveloped by impenetrable darkness!

Proud and ferocious Germany is visibly condemned, but the convulsions of that monster and the cataracts of blood!... What hope for an ark[11] over such a deluge? And where are God's chosen ones to be preserved in it? Without a doubt, France has promises, being the one nation among nations for which all could be pardoned; but it has accounts to settle as high as the columns of the firmament, and it is terrifying to think what it must still endure! The carnage and the agonies of the present hour – are they anything else than a school of training for future martyrs, that is to say for Christians still capable of feeling the predestination of their baptism? No other explanation for so prodigious an eruption is acceptable.

The destruction of the cathedral and the city of Reims, bombarded through the criminal deafness of its archbishop, a member of the Sacred College, contemner and persecutor of the Mother of God who had wept *in opposition to* him on the mountain of La Salette; that abominable immolation of Joan of Arc's

---

[10]Visionary of Dulmen: Catherine Emmerich (1774-1824).

[11]ark: Noah's ark, but also a pun on (Joan of) Arc.

capital, on the 68[12] anniversary of the celebrated Apparition,[12] at the *same hour* when the Miracle had been fulfilled and under the *same liturgical circumstances*, – would it not be the sign of a Wrath that nothing will be able to contain any longer?

There was, there, a modest and fragile statue of the Heroine, around which the hurricane of shells has destroyed everything, without being able to touch it – as of yet – as if the Maid of France had something yet to do! Tomorrow, maybe, we will learn that it has been pulverized in turn by the implacable disobedience of that pontiff. *Religio depopulata.*[13]

---

[12]68th anniversary day... Apparition: a reference to September 19, 1846 when Mélanie Calvat and Maximin Giraud saw the Marian apparition at La Salette.

[13]*Religio depopulata*: Latin for "ravaged religion" or "religion has been ravaged." The pontiff referred to is Pope Benedict XV: see *On the Threshold of the Apocalypse.*

Chapter 1: Jesus Christ's Lieutenant

The year of grace, 1422, on October 21, day of the Eleven Thousand Virgins, *perilous day*, according to the ideas of the Middle Ages, His Majesty, the very Christian and very fallen King Charles VI passed away in Paris, in his Hôtel Saint-Pol. Two years earlier, that unbalanced monarch, forgetting that he had an able son to succeed him, had abdicated in effect in favor of the king of England, by constituting him his heir, unheard-of extravagance desired by the despicable German woman who shared royalty with him for thirty-five years and had given him twelve children of uncertain provenance.

The intruding successor, deceased several weeks earlier, had no doubt made a sign to him from the bottom of his grave, for there had to be a mysterious connectivity between those two potentates of dream and illusion destined for the same worms and called to the same judgment. The German woman, with a reservation at the tribunal for infanticidal prostitutes, had to drag out her ignominious old age for another fourteen years.

A princely debauchery seasoned with some massacres in Flanders and elsewhere, followed by thirty-three years of dementia, – such was the sad reign of Charles VI. That king of France, formerly magnificent, gave up the ghost in a nearly deserted palace. The chancellor of France, the first chamberlain to the king, his confessor, his almoner, followed by a handful of subalterns: such were the witnesses of his last moments. The same material pomp was deployed for his funeral as for Henry of England. But no prince of the blood appeared at those lavish ceremonies. On the following November 10, the embalmed corpse was at first brought to Notre-Dame, then to Saint-Denis. Immediately behind the funeral cart, in its trajectory from Saint-Pol to the Cathedral, John, Duke of Bedford, walked alone, on foot. Then came the authorities and a multitude of people.

In their ignorant and *supernatural* affection, the people were more faithful to that king than the princes were. Paris, since the fourteenth century, was already what it has been ever since: a metropolis of opposition and the French capital of raillery. Vainly, under its eyes, Charles VI the Mad became the plaything of parties, the victor's booty. Vainly, during his reign and in the shadow of his throne, all disorders, all scourges, all miseries, including the shame of foreign yoke, came to weigh on the city and on the kingdom. The poor king never met with irony or insult. The most humiliating and most derisory of infirmities did not alter for one single day, in his venerated presence, the cult of monarchy.

On the day of his death, at the bedhead of her expiring spouse, Isabeau of Bavaria, Queen of France, was not at all to be found. On the day of his funeral, Philip the Good, Duke of Burgundy,[14] was absent. Not a son, not a relative. But the multitude of little people – whom that king had crushed – inundated the

---

[14]Philip the Good: who was Charles VI's brother.

capital. "And all the people who were in the streets
and in the windows wept and cried, as if each saw die
the thing they most loved." That day then, it seems,
there must have been some surprise in nature.

Notwithstanding those tears of an unfortunate
people, it was not the first time they shed them while
accompanying to the sepulture one of their pitiless
masters. The poor multitude believed perhaps that
they wept for the deceased. In reality, those humble
believers were weeping to see yet another of the
Thorns of the Sorrowful Crown of Jesus Christ disappear, vaguely divining or sensing in their hearts that
their number had been counted and that, in the end,
the Son of God would no longer have a crown on
earth.

Alone, of all the kings, the king of France
could be called his Lieutenant. However unworthy he
was or appeared to be, he was the indisputable interim
deputy of Christ, being seated on his throne to chase
away the devils. He seemed to heal the blind, the
mute, the deaf, the leprous, the paralytic, and to raise
the dead, certain images in ancient stained glass windows having appeared to attest to it, sometimes, in
very obscure chapels. There was no doubt that he had
the power to walk on water, if he had wanted to, having seen him often, on his war horse, making his way
through the blood of the dead. In any case, he multi-
plied admirably the lot of sorrow, and, when he gave
a terrible order, one thought one heard a parable from
the Gospel.

Jesus Christ's Lieutenant! as Joan understood
it, thus specifying the universal feeling in that waning

of the Middle Ages. Did anyone think to explain by Salic Law that magnificent Lieutenancy, exclusive and inalienable apanage of our kings? Jesus being the true Captain, it could not be that a woman might replace him in that completely divine magistery, which the holiest and most victorious knight would not have been worthy enough of. Simple and faithful souls understood that, and they almost did not see a mortal anymore in the least estimable king of France.

All those things are distant. That was adolescence then. In the absence of earthly joys, there were delights of intimacy with God, no longer familiar to modern peoples who had grafted onto the Tree of Knowledge the wild Stock of Death. But the memory of that springtime is not completely effaced, and when a poet expresses it, tears of ancient love surge still from some solitary hearts...

With Henry V dead and his son barely ten months old, John the Duke of Bedford was regent of France. That iniquitous English prince, impure and brutal like a twentieth-century Prussian, had been appointed by infallible Providence the constant and unfortunate adversary of Joan of Arc whom he could not get rid of except by assassinating her. But before the miraculous appearance of that girl on a mission from God, he had only the lamentable fruit of Charles VI and his German spouse before him. And yet, it was a matter to ascertain whether the deceased king had engendered him or not. A revelation by the Saint was needed to dissipate that incertitude.

What a situation for that heir to the throne of France whom his enemies called derisively, but rather exactly, the king of Bourges! No soldiers, no money, even less character, "of small courage," said Chastelain, "and always afraid of a violent death," showing no liveliness except for pleasure and a sort of stupor in the face of court affairs and perils. The English were masters of Normandy and a large portion of western France, the Duke of Burgundy reigning over Flanders, and the most traitorous of lords, Georges de la Trémouille, reigning over his will. The insuccess of Cravant and above all the disaster of Verneuil weighed down on him. Vainly, being only the dauphin as yet, he had approved, if not commanded, the assassination of John the Fearless, assassin himself, violent usurper of power and instigator of the civil war; who had no fear, in 1416, to negotiate at Calais with Henry V, victor of Agincourt, thus unleashing on the kingdom the shame and the scourge of invasion. That execution of an audacious blackguard, which only lacked judicial formality, had succeeded in compromising the young prince, while removing the king of England's most formidable competitor to the throne, and had given way to the execrable Treaty of Troyes, which made France English.

One hundred years later, in 1521, François 1st, passing through Dijon, visited the Chartreuse, ancient cemetery of the ducal house of Burgundy. That king of France, descendant of Louis, Duke of Orleans, brother of Charles VI, assassinated in 1407, wanted to contemplate in person the mortal remains of John the Fearless, the assassin of his forebear, who was transported there after his slaughter on Montereau Bridge. On seeing the frightening crack that cut into the skull of the duke, François 1st, expert in cuts and thrusts, cried out over the enormity of that wound. "*Sire*," said the Carthusian monk who accompanied him, "*it is through that hole that the English entered into France.*"

If there can be an excuse for Charles VII's debility of soul, he who was called the *Victorious*, because others, – and what others! – had reconquered the kingdom for him; that hyperbolic, cardinal excuse for the most revolting stagnation and darkest ingratitude, – one must look for it first at his beginnings as the child of a fool and a prostitute, then at the bloody whirlwind of monstrous incoherences that enveloped him from the cradle.

Born February 21, 1403, in the royal Hôtel Saint-Pol, the child prince soon had his apartments or *quartier* of habitation very close by, at the Hôtel du Petit-Musc – or *Pute-y-muce* – the name itself being sufficiently evocative.[15] The little Count de Ponthieu, – such was his title until the day his older brothers' death made him Dauphin – lived his first years then enveloped in an atmosphere of elegant orgies whose memory he retained and whose lessons he practiced into his ignoble old age. But other images were presented to his childhood.

Assuredly, he did not see the cutting of the throat or, to express it better, the pork butchery of his uncle d'Orleans, chopped alive by order of John the Fearless, but he must have heard the enormous clamor that ensued and the horrifying storm of civil war that resulted from it. Interested witness or spectator to

---

[15]*Pute-y-muce*: *Pute* means prostitute, and *muce* is possibly a reference to mucus.

the frightful rivalry between the Armagnacs and the Burgundians, he saw, from afar and at close range, the abomination of Cabochien[16] precursors to the horrible killers of September '92,[17] and the even greater abomination of the invasion of his inheritance by the English who arrived like crows, drunk still on the enormous carnage of Agincourt.

Having grown up and in order to inaugurate his adolescence, he had the Duke of Burgundy assassinated at Montereau, in reprisal perhaps for the recent massacre of the Armagnacs, but certainly to put an end to the palinodes of that bad man who could, from one moment to the next, hand France over to foreigners. Then he found himself in the presence of Henry V, of Bedford, and his frightening mother. Panic vision!

Sustained all the same by the military audacity of several impassive types like Dunoi the Great Bastard, Richemont, d'Alençon, Poton de Saintrailles, and the fantastical Etienne de Vignolles nicknamed La Hire, he was so redoubtable, Charles VII pulled along miserably until the arrival of Joan of Arc, the which saw herself forced to pull him along with her in turn, like a cadaver, in the last march to the throne of France that she constrained him to mount. Nothing of

---

[16]Cabochien: name of a faction, based in Paris, composed of members of the butcher and skinner guilds, tradespeople, that had initially allied with John the Fearless and the Burgundians against the crown and against the Armagnacs.

[17]precursors... September '92: a reference to the abolition of the monarchy, the proclamation of the French First Republic, and all the turmoil that preceded and succeeded it, in September 1792.

the sort had been seen, nor will be seen, very probably. He was too much of a little runt for that great girl
of the people, and too much of the heroic Middle
Ages ended with her person.

When it was necessary to make that stagnant
king move, from whom nothing had been asked except the momentary sacrifice of his imbecilic diver-
tissements, without his so much as having to lift a
combatant finger, it was, for Joan, the beginning of
her martyrdom. Even after the miraculous lifting of
the siege of Orleans, after Patay, after Troyes, after
the prodigious event of his coronation, after which all
he had to do was extend his hand to take Paris and become master of France, he affects incertainty still,
takes counsel from two or three blackguards whom he
despises, and returns to his filth.

When Joan, hideously betrayed, is held captive finally by those who trembled on hearing her
name mentioned merely, Charles VII who could have
delivered her, by using a little of the enormous ascendent he owed to that marvelous child's exploits; that
king, fabricated by her out of the mud, whom an atom
of chivalry should have precipitated into the boldest
of actions to save her, – he did not take one step and
continued to stagnate under his La Trémouille till the
late day when he had to consent to her immolation by
that suborner of vomitation and opprobrium.

Georges Chastelain, the pompous historian of
the dukes of Burgundy, enemy, besides, of Joan of
Arc and France, has painted, in three words, a portrait
of Charles VII. "He had," he said, "three defects:
mutability (capriciousness), *diffidence* (mistrust), and

envy." Little does it matter that he had certain positive qualities in compensation. That suffices for the dishonor of a prince. Imagine those three vices alone in a laborer or a cobbler, and you will have the idea of a nasty man. If you want to add "immense pride" to that list, the coarse fellow becomes Wilhelm II all of a sudden.[18] Excellent dispositions for spending the rest of his life in the mud and filth, and Charles VII had his fill of it. To be honest, one cannot reproach him with great pride. Everything was small with that Lieutenant of Christ. But the defects pointed out by Chastelain suggested to him at least two incomparable iniquities: the incomprehensible abandonment of the Maid, who had given him his kingdom, and the monstrous trial of his creditor Jacques Cœur who had helped him out twenty times.

The only thing that remained of that puppet was the final putrefaction of Louis XV, who did not invent the Deer Park any more than canon powder. One is assured that that Lady of Beauty, Agnes Sorel, lifted his heart however slightly, something I find hard to believe. After the death of that stunning concubine, the *capricious* Lieutenant of the Son of God, enthroned by Joan of Arc and tormenter of Jacques Cœur, died in the arms of forty *honorable* girls whom he had attentively corrupted.

---

[18]Wilhelm II: the German Emperor (1859-1940).

Chapter 2: The Angelic One

According to the *bestiaries* of heraldic science, the Unicorn is a horse-goat white in color and immaculate. That intrepid beast has on its forehead, disguised as a horn, a marvelous and redoubtable sword. Gifted with rapid legs, it defies the hunter's pursuits and his murderous attempts. But if, in the clearing of the woods, some girl should meet it in passing, suddenly the Unicorn stops. It obeys the voice of the virgin, lays its white head humbly in her lap, and lets itself be taken easily by that child's weak hands.

The Unicorn being the *support* of old England's coat of arms, some people adapted that legend to Joan of Arc's miraculous story. I'm not against it; but the immaculate whiteness of that animal of dreams – which really exists, one is assured, in the unexplored mountains of Burma – irks me a bit. So pure a coat attributed to England disconcerts me, and I also do not see that proud nation letting itself be dominated by innocence.

The English were, in the fifteenth century, what Wilhelm II's Germans are still today, ferocious and pillaging brutes, inaccessible to any generosity, to any kindness, to any justice, invulnerable in their pride as pachyderms, as incapable of an act of chivalry as of a rudimentary discernment of Beauty or of Greatness, execrable ravenous beasts that must be destroyed or expulsed by all means at hand. All the

same, that legend remarkably expresses the supernatural décor and the force of influence that the Middle
Ages attributed to virginity.

"In Joan of Arc's time," said a historian, "and
in many provinces of *France*, strictly speaking, there
reigned a very notable custom. When those who were
condemned to death were walking to their execution,
it happened betimes that some girl, seeing the proces-
sion pass, felt moved by a devout compassion. In that
case, she publicly laid claim to one of the miserable
wretches so as to make him her husband. That appeal
was suspensive; it immediately entailed the suspension of execution. Soon letters from the prince, in the
form of an act of remission, abolished the crime and
the punishment given. One can cite an authentic se-
ries of averred and numerous acts of that kind. It was
public knowledge finally that the Devil could do
nothing to a woman or girl while she was a virgin."
And that marvelous privilege could be communicated
by her, in the form of a plenary remission, to any
brigand whomsoever she was pleased to choose.

The man chosen by the Maid was the king of
France, not to marry him, but so that he might at least
become a man and not fail in his fate as a victor by
procuration, a sort of miracle that the chroniclers of
flesh and filth have not failed to attribute to Agnes
Sorel, fifteen years after the heroine's holocaust.

Joan's companions and contemporaries had
nicknamed her the *Angelic One*, and Dunois, the
proud Bastard of Orleans, was not afraid to declare
that he saw something divine in her. That something
subdued, incredibly softened those hardened riders of

the Hundred Years War. The coarsest and most violent among those men, La Hire himself, was subjugated. She obtained from him what a complete English army and the menace even of death could not have done: that he renounce his cursing or imprecations. One knows that furious girl's prayer at the moment of battle: "God, I beg you: let me do today for La Hire as much as you would want La Hire to do for me, if he were God and you La Hire." And "he tried his best," adds the chronicler, "to pray and speak well."

Probably he had his reasons, God not asking any more from machines of war. *Enfant terrible* of battles, unable to do without *swearing* at every instant, which, it appears, is indispensable for winning, Joan knew how to constrain him through gentleness not to curse in her presence except *by her stick!*

As for order or right, duty or obedience, such notions never entered the mind of that warrior. Would to God, however, that others had resembled him! La Hire, almost alone, accepted the Maid in good faith and without base envy, distinguishing himself in that regard from certain "colder" captains "and more tempered Lords," whose hideous jealousy hounded the saintly girl to death.

Joan of Arc is incomprehensible without Supernaturalness. She was not only a very pure virgin. Her purity was infectious, aggressive, illuminating like a living flame. The most impenitent *mercenaries* became chaste while looking at her. She could sleep tranquilly in their midsts, like a dazzling "dove with silvered wings" as is mentioned in Psalms.[19] The testimonies in that regard are unequivocal and surprising.

When the persecutors of Saint Lucie, exasperated by her vow of virginity which turned her body, she said, into a temple of the Holy Spirit, wanted to drag her by force to a place of prostitution, the Holy Spirit, according to *The Golden Legend*,[20] made her so heavy that a thousand men and fifty pairs of bull could not budge her.

To constrain Joan, the forces of the universe would not have sufficed. England wore itself out, got crushed, dishonored itself, and it is only today, barely, that the length of five long centuries and the surpassing prodigy of German iniquity can attenuate the memory of the frightening crime committed at the place du Vieux-Marché. What made Joan then so heavy for the English was, in her person, the weight of consciousness of an entire nation elected by God for the highest manifestations of His Glory, the weight of a kingdom that appeared heavier than the earth, and that the sun of Paradise shined on!

The historic figure of the Maid resembles an infinitely sweet and pure stained-glass window of the Annunciation, which the times and barbarians would have respected. It is the azure of France, and the color of fire of her punishment gently softened around that figure of a martyr. By the effect of a sublime confu-

---

[19]Psalms 68:13.

[20]The Golden Legend: compiled and published sometime in the 13th century, the *Legenda aurea*, by Jacobus da Varagine, was a collection of stories about the saints.

sion, she appeared to be at one and the same time the annunciator angel and the very obedient virgin humbly receiving the redoubtable sword that had to replace her pretty spinner's distaff. She does not understand at first what is asked of her. She does not know the history of France, she does not know either war or dreadful politics. She does not know anything, save that God suffers in his people and that there is a great feeling of pity for the Kingdom that was chosen in the past, since the time of his sorrowful Passion, during the paschal night, when the *Cock* began crowing. Then she rises tranquilly, resolutely, like a good girl of God and, guided by her Voices, becomes immediately an invincible strategist, leader of the highest princes and their infallible counsellor. After she has delivered France, the only thing she needs is to be delivered herself from her mission and, because she participates in the Holy Spirit, that other, more glorious deliverance cannot be achieved except by fire, after the preliminary horrors of the most infamous trial that has ever terrified men since the ineffable trial of Our Lord Jesus Christ!

The world never stops, it always keeps going. Immemorial, secular progression of the strong and the oppressed, of the iniquitous and the innocent whom they crush down, towards the communal grave of Eternity. History is merely a cry of grief throughout the centuries. It is as if there had not been a Redemption. One would be tempted to believe it if, every now and then, marvelous creatures did not appear who seem to say that the All Powerful is captive for an indeterminate period of time, that Supreme Justice is provisionally enchained, and that men of goodwill must trust in their God. Prefigurative creatures of consolation and hope, by their actions, of an unimaginable magnificence that the Scriptures announced.

At the hour I write these lines, the sun of France is hideously contaminated by heretical barbarians rather like the Arian Vandals of Genseric,[21] next to whom the classical brutes of Attila or Alaric resembled sheep. Systematic extermination of populations and cities, with the accompaniment of the worst cruelties.

The old historian Lebeau, recounting the invasion by those demons from the Roman provinces of Africa, expressed himself like this: "Their blind fury destroyed at first what they aspired to possess as a consequence, and they began the establishment of their empire by creating *a vast desert*. The most smiling and fertile country in the universe, populated by flourishing towns, was destroyed by iron, fire, and famine. No one was shown mercy." They also called themselves friends of God, declaring that an internal force drove them.

At a distance of fifteen hundred years, what a precise vision of the German war! The English of the fifteenth century, not yet heretical, were much less abominable than our Lutheran Prussians today. But they wanted the kingdom of Jesus Christ that sent a child against them, a totally angelic girl, to make them understand that that was really impossible. Today's unbridled heretics will be expulsed in their turn, and in a frightening fashion, not by a visible virgin

---

[21]Genseric: the leader and king of the Vandals and Alans, who famously sacked Rome in 455 AD.

feeble by nature, but by another All-Powerful and invisible Virgin whose miraculous intervention Joan of Arc prefigured.

It is true that France, today, is nearly Godless, and that we must submit, in punishment for our infidelities, to the throes of the present hour, without prejudice for the tribulations of agony that can surface after this war, if one does not correct his ways – which is, alas! very unlikely.

Jesus Christ, however, cannot be vanquished nor thwarted. He will come then Himself, if he has no one else any longer to send in his place, and that will be the Coming hoped for by all those burning with Love, the glorious and unrevealable Coming!

Chapter 3: The Miracle

That would be a misunderstanding of the history of France, in the first third of the fifteenth century, to suppose a simple duality of sentiments or influences, a normal antagonism more or less violent between France and England. There was an evil greater than the invasion itself, and the Duke of Bedford who, since the death of his brother, Henry V, governed the half-conquered kingdom, knew it all too well.

To quote Alain Chartier, France was "like a sea where each lord has as much seigniory as he has strength." There was a profound anarchy, with uncountable waves, always agitated, always menacing, and teeming with emergent monsters, with the furies that no powerful dike opposed.

Men of war, before Joan's arrival, were ignorant of discipline. There were disparate bands, lacking cohesion, of undulating temper, incapable of constancy, and rebellious to a single chief's impulsion. The chiefs themselves, not recognizing a superior authority, did not always succeed in making themselves obeyed. Princes of the blood, and experienced generals, had tried in vain to transform those free bodies, spread out and divided, into a true army of defense. At Orleans even, Dunois failed to dominate the rivalries and discords. One sees its effect on the famous Battle of Herrings,[22] an easy battle to win and stupidly lost, after which Orleans was on the verge of despair.

---

[22]Battle of Herrings: a battle near Orleans, between the French and the English, on February 12, 1429.

There was absolutely no national army. The soldiers, for the most part, were levied from abroad. There were the Scottish, whom their hatred for England and an instinct for pillage had drawn to France. Each year, vessels went to recruit those adventurers. There were also the Lombard archers attached to the Valentine house of Milan, the Aragonese, the Gascons, the Armagnacs, not one of them French, but rather Douglas, Stuart, and Visconti.

The sad king had placed his confidence in them, and those mercenaries, poorly paid moreover, great pillagers and rapists of women, who lived cruelly on the land, were not really what would have been needed to win the sympathies of the nation to his cause. Setting thatched cottages, villages, monasteries, cities, towns even, on fire; for such men it was war, just as it was for the Prussians of 1914, who were better equipped. Crushing children to death, mutilating young men, brutalizing young women, honorable women, and cutting them to pieces, violating religious, cutting the throat of old men; it was war. Breaking reliquaries and sacred vases, converting profaned churches into stables; it was war. The historical testimonies on that count are multiple, unanimous, irrefragable. It suffices to read the chronicles from that period... They exceed the most sombre of imaginations.

The rare, veritable defenders grouped around the person of the not-very-exciting monarch were scarcely much better than the insupportable foreigners, and Charles VII who was almost alone, and more and more the king of Bourges, saw the tiny portion of his realm that was still loyal to him melting away each day. The princes and provincial governors, indifferent to the distress of that declawed titular of supreme authority, acted with perfect independence, taking for themselves all that they could. The Count de Clermont in Auvergne, the Marshall de Séverac in Languedoc, comported themselves like sovereigns. The Count de Foix betrayed shamelessly. René d'Anjou, Duke de Bar and brother of the queen, negotiated with the English masters of the greater part of Champagne. It happened as if by maxim that, from the country of France, each lord took what he could conquer and keep. By consequence of such disorders, the people's misery was frightful and recalled the worst days of the preceding century.

One reads in the *Journal of a Bourgeois of Paris,* from the years 1419-1421: "You would have heard in all of Paris the pitiable lamentations, of small children, who cried: 'I'm dying of hunger!' One saw on a dungheap twenty, thirty children, boys and girls, who gave up their soul for hunger and thirst. Death was cutting so much and so quickly that it was necessary to dig large graves in the cemeteries where they put thirty or forty arranged like strips of bacon and barely sprinkled with earth. Those who dug the graves affirmed that they had interred more than one hundred thousand people. The cobblers took a tally, the day of sodality, of the deaths in their profession, and they found them to have exceeded eighteen hundred, as many masters as apprentices, in those two months. Packs of wolves ran through the countryside and entered Paris at night to remove the cadavers... Laborers said to each other: "Let's scram into the woods with the ferocious beasts... Adieu women and children... Let's do the worst we can do... Let's put ourselves into the devil's hand!" And it was the same story just about everywhere.

"No nation has fallen more before death," said Michelet. France already appeared to be dead. The four horses of the Apocalypse, the White, the Red, the Black, and the Pale, had galloped over it with their terrifying knights. The first armed with the redoubtable Bow and completely dazzling with its crown of victors; the second brandishing the exterminating Sword; the third, more terrible still, holding in one hand the Scale of Justice; the fourth finally, on the pale horse, Death itself, followed by Hell. In poor churches, not yet set on fire or profaned, blasts of fear and despair came from the exterior. So many arms twisted above their heads! So many sobs and tears at the foot of altars, of all the old saints of France, asleep for centuries, and what a pity in all that kingdom which they had stopped protecting!... *Et clamabant voce magna, dicentes: Usquequo, Domine?*[23]

It is said that death is the separation of the soul from the body. A commonplace that habit makes seemingly clear and which is absolutely incomprehensible. *Non est mortua, sed dormit*: "Why cry and trouble yourself? That young girl is not dead, but sleeping," said the Lord, and he resuscitates the Synagogue chief's daughter. Where was it, the soul of that child? Where was the soul of France whose body lay like cadavers and which was believed dead when

---

[23]*Et... Domine*: Latin for "And they clamored in a loud voice, saying: 'How much longer, Lord?'"

it was only sleeping?

The soul of France was at Domremy, and its name was Joan of Arc.

Chapter 4: "Dii estis"[24]

Joyous, adolescent, magnificent soul! The surprise and fear of the English were inexpressible. France was judged null and void, if not completely defunct, and then she appeared, blinding with youth.

No nation had been seen like that, at any time. England itself which intended to dominate it, did not remember being young, being a bastard issue of very old peoples whose decrepitude it had carried while giving birth. But this one now seemed, almost, not of this world, and one could believe her "without father or mother, without genealogy, without beginning and end," like the mysterious king of Salem whom Saint Paul "likened to the Son of God."

Truly supernatural apparition, that shepherdess of Domremy who incarnated France and who was not supposed to get old! "It is not possible," said the English, "that that girl belongs to humanity! She is a creature of the Devil! She is a sorceress!" And they remained obstinate in that thought, refusing to believe that one could be so young and so invincible.

In the same way, today, the mortal deception of Germany, too senile and too oafish however to believe in the demons that clearly possess it. The murderous renegade is surprised to find an adolescent and redoubtable France that it presumed broken by old age. There is something there that it cannot wrap its head around, but the barbarous rage that pushed it to

---

[24]*Dii estis*: Latin for "You are gods."

destroy the city of Reims betrays its most significa-
tive disquietude.

Instinctively, without knowing and without
understanding, – as animals of the desert can sense,
from a great distance, a source of fresh water that
they will dig up – the German brutes hurled themselves at that marvelous Basilica which was, at one
time, the heart of France, when Joan of Arc had her
king coronated there. Of course, that was five hundred years ago, and Joan of Arc has moved on, following the example of the "sparrow that migrates into
the mountain." There is no king either. The kings
have disappeared by descending to the level of the
crowds. No matter, there was then perhaps, for those
devastating bison, some precious remnant of that
elixir of long life and eternal youth that surprised the
English. It was necessary that it stop existing and that
Joan be killed anew, killed by fire, if that was even
possible.

But the Maid is the imperishable passiflora,
and she will not pass away any more than the Word
of God will. The barbarians will finish perhaps by understanding that finally, when the fire that they have
so cruelly abused will turn against them, shedding
light on their atrocious faces, and the undying face of
the virgin whom they insulted.

That exclusive privilege of France is a mystery. Whatever might be its infidelities or its crimes, it
is redivivus under the knife of punishment... Consider
that then and think on it! God has nothing but France!
If France perished, Faith would subsist somewhere
else perhaps, even if in a corner of the North Pole,

with shivering Charity, but there would be no more Hope!...

Time is an imposture of the Enemy of humankind that the perenniality of souls despairs of. We are still in the fifteenth century, as in the tenth, as at the central hour of the Immolation on Calvary, as before the advent of Christ. We are really in each one of the folds of the multicolor apron of ancient History. In spite of death, we are eternal, in a way, being Gods, as it is affirmed: *Ego dixi: Dii estis*.[25] If one does not think of France, what does that Word of the Holy Spirit mean? Humanity is explicable and plausible only through France. *Arbor de fructu suo cognoscitur*.[26] It is the fruit of the tree of nations. Everything was done for France, in order that one day everything would be done by France.

The Jewish race which was formerly God's People and which still is in a mystical sense, being, by nature, sacerdotal and inherent in Holiness, just as the accident is to the substance; the Jewish race, having become penitent the world over, surprises the earth after twenty centuries by its persistence and verminous paralysis, while waiting for the hour when its First-born will command it to rise up and carry its "low bed" into its house. But France is a secretly adoptive child preferred forever and which will never have need of a low bed, not having known paralysis.

She has deep roots everywhere; in ancient

---

[25]*Ego dixi*: Dii estis: Latin for "I said: You are gods." Psalms, 82:6-8.

[26]*Arbor... cognoscitur:* Latin for "The tree is known by is fruit."

Asia, in hypogeal Egypt, in the caves of Thessaly, in the catacombs of Rome, probably even at the bottom of swallowed-up Atlantis and under the impenetrable massifs of lost Eden. She remembers having adored and broken all her idols, including her own image, being simultaneously indocile and spiritual, mutinous and repentant, like those children of love who are difficult to punish.

She has been punished, however, severely punished sometimes. She is punished today, she will be tomorrow, very probably, and the *Arm* that will fall on her will be heavier than the atrophied arm of the German emperor. No matter, all will be pardoned in the end, because she has loved much more than another and her radiant youth is as irresistible as her courage.

What could they possibly have against a nation that gave birth to Joan of Arc, the villainous horde that blossomed the day before yesterday on the Lutheran dungheap and which, several days from now, will be nothing more than a mountain chain of rotting carcasses? A worse danger threatens it, and the greatest miracle will not be great enough to preserve it. It is absolutely necessary, you know, O glorious Christ! the plenary amnesty of that Madeleine from the Garden of Resurrection being as necessary to your magnificence as the equilibrium of the firmament!

Chapter 5: The Epic

This book does not want to be, and cannot be, the history of Joan of Arc, a history that is hidden or shamefully denatured over the course of four centuries, a little better known now but only after the sixty years of serious research that Jules Quicherat was the initiator of. Curious people who instruct themselves thoroughly may consult the bibliography located at the end of this present volume. It will suffice for me to give a rapid sweep of it in broad strokes.

"In the fourteenth and fifteenth centuries," said Siméon Luce, "the chatelaine of Vaucouleurs, hemmed in between the seigneury of Commercy to the north, the Barrois in the west and to the south, and Lorraine to the east, which is separated from it by the Meuse river, comprised a certain number of scattered villages on the left bank, along the ancient Roman road that winds from Langres to Verdun at the foot of a small chain of hills or knolls covered on their crest at that time by forests, already planted with vineyards on the slopes, and surrounded by the lush green prairies of the Meusean valley. The village of Domremy, Joan of Arc's hometown, composed the extreme south of that chatelaine buried as it were between a corner of Lorraine and Barrois. At the beginning of the fourteenth century, it had belonged to a cadet branch of the illustrious Champenoise family of Joinville. But, in 1335, an arrangement with Philippe VI occurred, by virtue of which that chatelaine was ceded to the king of France... Thirty years later, in 1365, Charles V gave order that the chateau and the

villages belonging to Vallois would from that moment forward be an integral part of the royal domain
and would be attached inseparably, irrevocably, and
directly to the crown of France."

Joan of Arc, born in 1412, was then French
and of truly French extraction.

The Catholic faith was alive and well in that
area, and the young Jeannette, as she was called, began her astonishing life by assiduousness in prayer as
practiced by the humble folk and little people. The
house of her parents was contiguous with the cemetery, little-known circumstance that would explain
perhaps the remarkable depth of her piety and that
touch of melancholy, which is particular to the greatly
predestined, whose joyous humor of an innocent often
appeared distorted. The strongest roots of that sovereign soul must have been among the dead.

One reads, in a deposition of Dunois at the trial of rehabilitation, that Joan had, one day, a vision
wherein she saw Saint Louis and "saint" Charlemagne who were praying to God for the salvation of
King Charles VII and for the deliverance of Orleans.
She didn't tell the whole story and, clearly, she could
not tell all, but one can suppose that the heart of that
eminent virgin was like a cathedral where the hum-
blest as well as the greatest of the dead came to chant
first vespers for the blessed day of Deliverance.

When the war, which was everywhere at that
time, brought murder and arson into the valley of the
upper Meuse, and when Joan saw with her own eyes
the frantic flight of poor fellow citizens seeking

refuge among their beasts in the neighboring citadel, she felt the kingdom's great misery, a superhuman clarity developed within her and around her, and she heard Voices from heaven. The archangel Saint Michael, appointed protector of France and Valois in particular, subsequently the great Auxiliary Saints Marguerite and Catherine, appeared to her, saying that she needed to leave her parents and village and go on behalf of the king of Heaven to the king of France who would give her warriors with which she could deliver Orleans. – "Go! girl of God, go! The gentle dauphin is the true blood of France!"

At that epoch, prior to the coronation, Charles was still rather commonly designated by the title of Dauphin. There was even here and there, and in the heart of that prince, an agonizing doubt on the legitimacy of his birth.

Surprised at first and naturally frightened by such a mission, the poor little shepherdess understands that she must obey. Rebuffed two or three times by Baudricourt, the rude Captain of Vaucouleurs, she succeeded, after weeks of humiliation and internal gnawing, by obtaining an escort. "I have come here," she said to Jean de Metz who was one of her traveling companions, "because this here is the *King's Chamber*, because Vaucouleurs is a royal town, so that Robert de Baudricourt will want to lead me or have me led to the king, but he does not heed my words. And nevertheless I must present myself to the king, even if I should wear my legs down to the knees, for nothing in the world, not the king, nor the duke, nor the King of Scotland's daughter, can recov-

er the kingdom of France, and there is no other recourse save me. Certainly, I would love nothing better
than to stay home spinning with my poor mother, because it's not my station; but I have to go and I must
do it, because God wants me to."

She departs with six respectable and devout
companions who believed in her. But what a voyage!
Nearly 150 leagues, including detours, in a territory
under war, cut off by water courses, bristling with
garrisons, and half of it in enemy hands. Alone, the
Maid shows herself inaccessible to every feeling of
fear, and when someone speaks to her of the dangers
she will run, she responds with assurance that she has
a clear path before her, and that if the enemy is met
and wants to stop her, her Lord God will know best
how to free the way to the Dauphin whom she must
have coronated. "It's what I was born for," she said
on every occasion. They arrive, in fact, at Chinon
without event, on the eleventh day. The magnificent
tribulations were about to begin.

First she had to obtain an audience, and that
was not easy. Charles VII, throughout his life, had as
a dominating character trait, written on his face and in
his eyes, mistrust. Although young yet, that ailment
of the soul was already, with him, very pronounced.
After meticulous questioning and deliberation for
three days, he consented to receive her, but not one on
one. Everyone knows the first test: the king hiding
among his lords all dressed in sumptuous costume,
and Joan, who had never seen him before, going
straight up to him unhesitatingly.

"Gentle *daulphin*," she says, "I am named Jehanne la Pucelle, and the king of heaven sends me, that you, by me, might be coronated and crowned in the city of Reims." And immediately she confirms the surprising authority of that phrase by telling confidentially to the king, on the part of God, the most precise response to one of his prayers, that nobody could have known about.

In one hour of extreme anguish, having learnt that the English were about to assault Orleans, last stakes of the crown of France, and thinking of his mother Isabeau's proverbial shame, he had asked in the privacy of his oratory that if he was truly the *legitimate* heir of the throne, then the God of saint Charlemagne and Saint Louis should manifest it to him clearly. Nothing more conclusive than the messenger's miraculous perceptiveness. "*I tell you,*" said Joan with grandiose simplicity, "*I tell you, on behalf of My Sire, that you are the true heir of France and the son of the king.*"

Charles could no longer hesitate. But that did not suffice. It was necessary that no one might doubt Joan's mission. It was necessary that she be examined and interrogated, at Poitiers, by the most renowned bishops and doctors of the church. New and crucifying delay for the saintly daughter whose heart bled while imagining the besieged city's distress. "Time weighs on me like a woman about to become a mother!" she groaned. Finally, after three weeks, the examiners declared that they were satisfied, they went about equipping her, putting together a military entourage, assigning a *station* to her and a command, then sending victuals and munitions through her to

Orleans. The preparation for the expedition lasted another month almost. The Leader of war was about to
appear.

At this point, human reason fails. We are so
much in the presence of the inexplicable that even the
word *miracle* does not satisfy the mind. The instantaneous healing of a paralytic, the resurrection of a
deadman, the walking of a saint on the surface of wa-
ters can be conceived of as so many miracles. It is the
All Powerful who intervenes to put back in their place
the things that were no longer. But the sudden trans-
formation of a space within another space, of a lily in
an oak, for example, the fleet infusion, like a lightning bolt, the highest military genius in the mind and
heart of a little, innocent, peasant girl completely
lacking in all human knowledge, that is not conceiv-
able. Such however was the case with Joan of Arc in
April 1429.

It will soon be time to speak of her Voices, to
affirm that all her acts and even the least of them
were dictated to her as she went along, without her
needing to do anything else than obey. Joan of Arc
was not that instrument. Assuredly her Voices, sent to
her, gifts of God, had prescribed to her the expulsion
of the invaders, and the coronation of the king of
France. Without any doubt, they continually sustained
her will and comforted her until the last hour. It is
even permitted to believe that at the supreme moment
the pitiable Auxiliary Saints who had followed her
with so much love since her infancy spared her the
atrocity of flames and carried her off completely
asleep into the fresh valley of Paradise. In that sense,

one can say that she was exceptionally privileged. But she had, in common with all human creatures, the intangible freedom of the children of God, the power to accomplish supererogatory acts *on her own*, even though they were enveloped in eternal Prescience. Incontestably, she always wanted what God wanted, but she wanted it *in her way* which was nobody else's in the world. One calls that *genius* because it is incomprehensible and because the word does not mean anything. One is forced then to suppose in Joan of Arc, at the same time with Sanctity, a spontaneous blossoming of that indefinable faculty. And that there is what is completely incomprehensible.

When the military genius of Bonaparte revealed itself, one was astonished doubtless, but one did not feel oneself absolutely in the presence of a prodigy. He had already shown something of it, and those who entrusted him with the poor army of Italy considered him a remarkable officer at the least. Nothing of the sort for Joan of Arc. Imagine, by analogy, Michelangelo's *Moses* or Beethoven's *Missa solemnis* conceived and executed, from one day to the next, by a man not only devoid of all artistic culture, but ignorant even that art exists and that the means and resources cannot be guessed at. That is however what happened with Joan of Arc, not once and by the effect of one of those encounters that would have always been considered entirely improbable, but everywhere and at all times, infallibly, and it is enough to boggle the mind.

Just yesterday she was innocently spinning beside her mother and knew about nothing else. Today

she calmly declares that she is going to deliver Orleans to start with, Orleans that is being besieged, for
seven months now, by a formidable army, which the
most renowned captains despair to hold on to for the
king, and which is about to be surrendered. And she
does what she says. Orleans is delivered by her *in
four days*. Immediately afterwards, it is the lightning
bolt campaign of the Loire, the marvelous battle of
Patay more incredible than the victory of the Pyramids, all the walls falling down then before her and,
several days later, the Basilica of Reims, the coronation of Charles VII which annulled forever the execrable Treaty of Troyes.

Joan of Arc's Voices had announced all that to
her. She knew it and spoke about it with certitude.
However, no visible miracle intervened to assure the
fulfillment of her prophecy. No flaming sword, no
labarum, no celestial army appeared to terrify or para-
lyze the enemy. The rank-and-file English soldiers
could believe in malefice, but their leaders who knew
war, having fought at Agincourt and elsewhere, for
thirty years, understood quite well, without avowing
it, that they found themselves in the presence of an incomparable military hability of strategy and tactic,
difficult knowledge that can only be acquired by hard
labor. That ignorant young girl exercised both the one
and the other against them, with perfect mastery, as
naturally as one breathes the air of the fields or the
mountains, and they conceived a profound irritation
which was, one day soon, going to cost the victorious
girl very dearly.

One day also, and even sooner, her unworthy

king was going to abandon her without defense to the abominable traitors whom he favored, and when Joan was disloyally taken, in the middle even of one of her most brilliant battles, the tormenters of France who held that sublime virgin in their impious hands finally could avenge themselves on her as basely and as cruelly as they were given to do, but they did not prevail, in their consciences, against the inexpressible superiority by which that admirable child had overcome their pride.

Chapter 6: The Warrioress

What has just been said puts us at an incredible distance from the sentimental imagery of boutiques of piety and the literary sweetshops of devout panegyrics. There is nothing so distant from Joan of Arc and all that martyr's acts as the confiture or colored paper of our religious decadence, to say nothing of the profaning imagination of Sulpician sculptors and stained-glass window makers. Divided between a mediocre desire to honor the Blessed One and the pudic fear of frightening away the heifers of devotion by exalting the warrioress, gossips and false artists have fabricated a Joan of Arc to suit themselves.

The Maid wore men's clothing which was necessitated by her life in camps; she rode a horse with surprising hability, without ever having had lessons, not as an Amazon huntress, but as a general commanding real soldiers; and she practiced real war where men are killed. Those things that she was grievously reproached for at Rouen by the prevaricative judges continue today to rile the scrupulous consciences of those who claim to venerate her, and they make their enthusiasm shiver. The cuirass mitigated by the skirt! that is what is required.

What would the postulators of that masquerade say if they knew everything? if the Joan of Arc of History they ignore appeared to them? What would their consternation not be like in the presence of such a fact as this: "Bastard! Bastard!" she said one day to Dunois, "in the name of God, I command you, as soon as you return from Falstaff you must let me know; for if it happens that I do not know it, I promise you – I will have your head cut off!" She never had the "head cut off" of one of her French captains, but she was known to be a woman of her word, and she was capable of doing what she said.

Certain people, thinking to arrange everything, would perhaps want that virile Maid of eighteen years not to have been a woman at all except in appearance, Jesus delegating in this way a sort of monster to save France. The cutthroat theologasters of Rouen wanted to have a clean conscience, and poor Joan had to submit to the most humiliating of examinations, by order of those pudibund Pharisees. She was every bit a woman however, and, beyond the acts of a warrior, she was easy to be moved to tears. But she was the ideal Woman, "ideal as never a poet has understood or will understand, so much does it exceed our conceptions." *Terribilis ut castrorum acies ordinata*,[27] says the canticle of love. *In interitu vestro ridebo et subsannabo*:[28] "I will laugh on your perdition and I will mock you when what you fear finally happens to you." Words that Solomon puts into the mouth of Wisdom itself, which is none other than Mary conceived without sin: the Queen of Virgins.

"My Lord possesses a book that no clerk reads, however perfect in clericature he might be." Response by Joan to her chaplain who told her that one cannot find in any book such actions as hers. Her

[27] *Terribilis... ordinata*: Song of Songs 6:9 (Vulgate)

[28] *In territu... subsannabo*: Proverbs 1:26

luminous innocence would elucidate for her that book of her Lord's, indecipherable for the most learned of savants. She read there what was expedient for her to know, and, without a doubt also, in the most enigmatic of characters, the dolorous future of her nineteenth year which had to be her last, for it is known that she had the gift of prophecy.

On the way to Reims where she had so much trouble bringing the king, wanting by all means that he hurry, she had said to that sad sire that she would not last longer than one year and that one should know well how to employ her, for she had much to do yet. One employed her as poorly as possible and, nevertheless, what didn't she do! There was not only the English to be chased out of France, there were the Burgundians to make submit. Enormous tasks that she was certainly capable of accomplishing, if *they* had not hampered her.

Impenetrable decrees opposed her. The king's discouraging inertia was not enough, the worst hostility of his venenous minsters who had the king's ear were needed, – and the hour had not sounded, it appears, – in order to despair completely of the Enemy of humankind. What Joan had begun and what she had achieved in twelve months, twelve years would be needed, after her, and incalculable combats to bring things to a conclusion. France was not yet rid of the English, and the tenacity of Louis XI was required to settle things, much later, with Burgundy.

Two adversaries, the Burgundian chroniclers Monstrelet and Chastellain have exposed, "with perfect simplicity," says the captain Paul Marin, that the

Burgundian army and the English army feared no other French leaders at Joan of Arc's stature. For the Burgundians, Joan was the *genius of the war*. That's not to say there was a penury of worthy captains among the French, but neither Dunois, nor La Hire, nor Saintrailles knew how to put together a battle plan, an operation of war, with the magistral clarity that Joan could. In the execution of a plan, none of those men had the hability to spot a weak point in the adversary, or to parry instinctively an unexpected failure in one wing of the army. Never has a captain, before Bonaparte, known how better to seize the moment; never has a general grasped in a more instantaneous manner the shortcomings of his adversary, his defective dispositions, and the means to extract from them the must stunning successes.

She excelled, her contemporaries said, in handling the lance, in forming squads, in making troops take up a position, in disposing artillery. Impossible to be any further away from the Domremy distaff, as these lines from an old Burgundian manuscript bear witness to: "She was a marvel at arms and handled a lance very powerfully and defended herself adroitly, as one saw on a daily basis." But those last qualities, however surprising they might be for a young girl, are accessory and do not surpass, militarily, her level of tactic. What precedes is what confounds reason and impresses the idea of a miracle.

At the battle of Patay, June 18, anticipatory anniversary of Waterloo, early in the morning, after having announced battle: "Are your spurs in order?" she said to the Duke d'Alençon. "Why?" he exclaimed, "are we planning to turn around and flee!" "Of course not, in the Name of God! The English, yes, they will turn. They will be discomfited without our hardly losing a man; and you will need good spurs to pursue them." It is the strategist who speaks like that with a bit of enjoyment. She knew what she was talking about, having seen and prepared everything in advance.

"It is the genius of the strategist," Paul Marin observed, "to drive the adversary back into a corner from which he cannot escape without resorting to a desperate tactical operation. That is the secret of the great captain to bring things to that point, just as it is the talent of a player of chess to deliver the fatal mate... Joan was an habile tactician and a first-rate strategist. Before the tactician prescribed the clash of arms, the strategist had the clear intuition of what was at stake. She went into battle after having calculated her advantage."

The majority of panegyrists of the Blessed One want to find her supernaturally gifted in order to lead troops, which is incontestable, but they want nothing else, and sentimental religiosity steps in immediately to make a caricature of that great figure. Honest devout people to whom images of piety suffice and who think they *know*, would be surprised to learn that Joan of Arc's acts of war were not an expansion of her enthusiasm, but the more or less spontaneous result, in appearance, of a powerful and grave thought. Clearly, it would be less difficult to conceive of that prodigy if one forgot that she was a **Saint** and the predestined schoolgirl of Saint Michael, the strategist of heaven's armies, who had taught her how to read in a very mysterious book. When, with a voice that has pierced five centuries and that I still hear, Joan cried to her men: "Go inside! *It's yours!*" she expressed, doubtless, with a perfect confidence in God; but at the same time she spoke as the leader of an army who had anticipated everything, everything settled on in advance, and who knew exactly what she needed to say.

To be precise, let's cite again the excellent military historian of Joan of Arc, the captain of artillery Paul Marin, with respect to his heroine's bold stroke. It has to do with a night attack.

"One must not believe that an attack of this kind is easy. One must have, to organize a strike under similar conditions, a set of rare qualities. One knows the considerable importance of the operation of security and the operation of discovery. For every serviceman who has reflected on multiple operations of war, nothing is rarer than the set of qualities by which an officer can bring to successful conclusion the operation of discovery he is charged with. It's even worse if the responsibility of commander in chief devolves on that same chief of patrol. It is in constatation of that difficulty that military writers must have given a place of honor to the memory of the Lasalles, the Curélys, the Montbruns, those admirable partisan leaders on whom the security of the army relied, who vanquished at Arcole, at the Pyramids, at Jena! Joan of Arc had that set of qualities to the highest degree. In the numerous operations of war to which her name remains eternally bound, fifteenth-century chroniclers have discovered neither a fault nor an error. As for the emeritus captains who fought in Joan of Arc's company: the Dunois, the La Hires, the Saintrailles, they recognized the Maid's military ascendant, to the point of considering her, in battles and in councils, like a captain more prudent and wise than the most experienced amongst them.

"Joan's status in the eyes of those great warriors of the fifteenth century, – it is indispensable to recall it for people who have not read their declarations. That so extraordinary status is more eloquent than all the eulogies of Joan given by writers of our time. As for the appreciation by Burgundian or English chroniclers who had heard mention of her by witnesses to her actions, it constitutes later a most precious document from the point of view of the heroine's military merit. Take the recorded memory of the greatest of captains, that of Napoleon. Was it not repeated by more than one of his marshals that at Moscow the emperor lacked decision, and that he had also slept too much! As far as concerns Joan of Arc, not a word of that kind was mentioned by the French marshals who served under orders of the young girl, formerly a shepherdess having become an army chief overnight. The fact is there was nothing to talk about. Joan of Arc's attitude imposed respect on all her captains, her subordinates, and her companions. With her, no personal preoccupation of the sort that took away Napoleon's freedom of mind, when he did not dare launch, at the decisive moment, the imperial guard, last guarantee of his own security. With Joan of Arc, no place for sleep, no place for physical rest when the hour of action had sounded. The memorable

examples of her assault on Saint-Honoré's Gate and
her assault on the Tourelles, the no less beautiful example of Joan beating a retreat with her troops to the
boulevard de Compiègne (where she was traitorously
seized) – all demonstrate the evidence that she was
not concerned for her body or for her personal safety
when it was a matter of winning the battle. Joan was
the first soldier of France, the first soldier as well as
the first strategist and the first tactician."

I have previously mentioned how humanly inexplicable that is. One cannot insist too much on it,
for that is the astonishment of the centuries. But one
must insist even more on the absolutely dominating
fact of Joan of Arc's *saintliness,* which is unique and
resembles no other saintliness.

In a general way, that marvelous state is always a visible and sensible manifestation of divine
Glory. It is a certain return to the primordial Integrity
that preceded the Fall, but with the colossal compli-
mentary Beauty that adjoins Sorrow to it. In particular, it is infinite diversity, each Blessed One needing
to possess the mark of a special Volition of the Holy
Spirit. In any case, it is conformant with our instinct
to group and to classify, to conjecture on the cate-
gories, swarms of the analog elect lacking in absolute
identity, nebulae of triumphant parasites separated
from each other by unknown immensities in the
unimaginable depths of Paradise.

Joan of Arc's saintliness excludes, on the contrary, any idea of a rapprochement or fusion, any hy-
pothesis of assimilation to a group. She is the giant of
saintliness. Her splendor is marvelously incompatible.

It pleased God to turn that little shepherdess spontaneously into a great captain, without ridding her of the simplicity of a damselfly from the Garden of Innocence; to arrange or to *reveal* in that way – because there is no other way to put it – an overwhelming antinomy for thought; and that monster of miracle that had never been seen since the Holy Spirit's incursion among men, we have nothing better to do than to subscribe to it in admiration while weeping, while telling ourselves that the Maid's infinitely exceptional and completely paradoxical saintliness was just what was needed for the birthing of an epic that defies all poetry, all sublunar comprehension.

Although military strategy is a human knowledge, it proceeds necessarily from God like everything else. It hung from the Tree of Temptation. In that sense, God is the infinite Strategist, and he makes it known well enough when he forces souls most hostile to him to give up the ghost. One day he judged it "worthy and just, equitable and salutary" to allocate to Joan of Arc that surprising gift because it corresponded mysteriously with that stage of election that is unknown to us and that we cannot even dream about. We will later discover that it was as simple and as hidden as the Parables contained in the Gospel. *Laus tibi, Christe!*[29]

---

[29]*Laus tibi, Christe:* Latin for "Christ be praised."

Chapter 7: The Prophetess

One can be a prophet without being a saint. That is evident. But it is impossible apparently not to be a prophet when one is a saint. Even then, when a saint does not announce future events, he is forced to pre-figure them and to configure them unbeknownst to himself by the precision of his attitudes or by his gestures. Joan prophesied, not only through words, but through acts. Intuition of another's thought; perception at a distance; prescience of the future; such were the three powerful faculties proclaimed at first by her expressions.

The first manifested itself by the revelation made to the king of an intimate secret that was between God and him, the secret of an anguished prayer that his confessor did not even know about; revelation that determined the hesitant will of that poor prince. The so well-known and so remarkable act of her recognition of the dauphin in the middle of the court was only the preliminary manifestation. Other proofs of that infallibility of intuition demonstrated, by what followed, that nothing could be hidden from that admirable girl.

Her too short life was filled with phenomena of perception at a distance. Around May 13, 1428, Joan wanted to write to Charles VII to tell him to keep himself well and not to enter into battle before Mid-Lent. It was a first prophetic warning. The fol-

lowing February 12, 1429, she said to Robert de Baudricourt: "In the name of God, you are taking too
much time to send me, for today the gentle dauphin
has suffered a great setback in Orleans, and the damage will be even worse if you do not send me immediately to him." That day then, six or seven thousand
French, having been led by the most valiant of captains, were put to flight by 1,500 English, having
hampered a long convoy of victuals. It is the well-
known day of the *Herrings*. From Vaucouleurs and at
the hour when that event took place, Joan saw Rou-
vray-Saint-Denis' defeat. An act of the same order is
the indication of the sword of Sainte-Catherine de
Fierbois, an astonishing act that almost all chroniclers
have mentioned.

The same prophetic flashes illumine the bat-
tlefields; in particular they direct the heroine's first
military operation. On May 4, 1429, Falstaff was
leading victuals and men to the English. Someone had
promised Joan that she would be alerted when the attack on that convoy began. But the action was engaged in without her being made aware of it. Mean-
while, d'Aulon, her equerry, who "was tired and
overworked," laid down on a small bed in the same
room as the young girl, "to rest a bit." Joan and her
hostess were sleeping as well in another bed. Suddenly a mysterious call wakens her. "In the name of
God!" she cried to d'Aulon, "my counsel has told me
that I must go against the English, but I do not know
if I must go against their strongholds or against Falstaff who has to re-victual them." Whereupon and
forthwith the said equerry got out of bed, and as
quickly as possible armed the said Maid. Then, de-

spite the distance, she knew that the soldiers were repulsed at the fortress of Saint-Loup, and addressing herself to d'Aulon, she said: "Ha! damn boy, you did not tell me that French blood had been spilt! Go get my horse." She rides towards the gate of Burgundy, "going as straight as if she knew the way beforehand," so quickly did the sparks fly from the pavement, and victory is the result of that sudden illumination.

That faculty of hers always served Charles VII's interests until the day his inertia was invincible. Surrounded by his ministers, he held many secret deliberations with them. Joan arrived infallibly in the midst of that discussion. "Stop with the interminable counsels," she said, "but act more quickly to proceed to your worthy coronation." Or even: "You have had your counsels, I have had mine. Now believe me when I tell you that the counsel of my Lord will hold and yours will dissolve." They took up the march forward, but it was always to start over again. Joan's spirit of prophecy was at one and the same time the illumination and the driving force.

There would be no end to it if one had to recount all the times her clear vision of the future manifested itself. From 1424, being only twelve years old then, she knew the secret of her vocation. But she did not reveal it until 1428. That was the dawn. In the month of May, one saw it: she declared to the sire de Baudricourt that he needed to send word to the dauphin that the Lord would assist him before Mid-Lent, that he would become king in spite of his enemies, that she herself would lead him to his coronation. Rebuffed at first and taken for a madwoman, she insists, she clarifies, saying that they were taking too long to send her, that already the prince had suffered greatly for that delay, and that he was in danger of an even greater setback. Intimidated, Baudricourt eventually ceded.

On their departure, the dangers of the trip are represented to her. "My path is clear," she responded. "In the name of God lead me to the king and have no doubt that nothing will stop me." For eleven days, Joan and her companions crossed English lines with impunity, regions where "all pillaging and robberies reign."

At Chinon, from the moment of her arrival, an incident occurred that shocked everyone. A roughneck soldier on horseback, seeing her pass, started shouting at her, sniggering and uttering blasphemies. "Ho!" she said, "in the name of God, you curse Him and you are so near to your death!..." That very evening, that man fell into the Vienne and drowned.

Having become general of the army, she wanted to enter besieged Orleans with a handful of soldiers from the right bank of the Loire, through the strongest of English strongholds. Through that point, Orleans was inaccessible; but she knew, independently of any rational thought, and she affirmed, that her troops would pass unscathed. The captains elaborated a plan; it did not matter, she saw correctly, and de Blois' army, in order to penetrate the city, was obliged to follow the route indicated by her. After having turned into a victory what had begun as a defeat before the fortress of Saint-Loup, she reanimated by her prescience the valiant men who had been fighting for seven months and announces solemnly that on the following Sunday, May 8, on the Feast of the Annunciation of Saint Michael, Orleans would be delivered and all the English would be routed.

On May 7, the decisive battle took place, and again it was her lucidity as a seer and her authority as an inspired leader that ensured a brilliant triumph. At the moment when the leaders, thinking all was lost, ordered a suspension of conflict, Joan affirmed their success "by many a beautiful and bold expression." "In the name of God," she said, "you will soon be inside. Have no doubt, the English will lack the strength finally... Go back, by God." That promise was all that was needed to lead the soldiers back, but then, says a contemporary, "never before had a group of little birds been seen like that to alight on a bush, every single one of them who gathered on that said boulevard."

Many circumstances of that memorable day had been prophesied as well: the death of Glasdale who had insulted her and who was drowned – "he died without bleeding," she said; the victorious reentry of the Orleanais over the bridge that was so long under Suffolk's control; finally the wound she received between the shoulder and the throat during that fight. The previous day, in fact, on May 6, she had said that "her blood would jet from her body above her breast." Already, for a month now, she had announced that wound to the dauphin.

She was now going to fulfill the promise of coronation. But it was necessary to clear the route and

behold the surprising campaign of the Loire. The
heroine conducted it with an impeccable military
knowledge and her continual prescience of contingents. She sees in advance the events, she knows the
success of operations and identifies "in the name of
God" the precise moment to act. Her intuitive virtue
shines on everything. At Jargeau, at Patay, she declares victory with supernatural authority. At Troyes,
there is talk of turning back to the Loire, the troops
were so discouraged by the resistance of that entirely
Burgundian city. "Gentle king of France," she said,
"if you wish to reside in front of your city of Troyes,
it will be yours within two days, either by force or by
love, and make no doubt about it." The following day
the city opened its gates, and the sublime warrioress
led the king to his "dignant coronation," assuring him
that the bourgeois of Reims, hostile until then, would
rally to him, which they did.

After that triumph, Joan felt that the hour of
abandonment was about to sound. On April 15, 1430,
she revealed with remarkable clairvoyance the dolorous mystery of her destiny. She would be taken prisoner before Saint John's Day. In fact, up until the fatal deadline, May 23, the saints spoke to her of that
hard trial. One of the wicked men who tortured her at
Rouen with their interrogations asked her, on March
1, 1431: "Have your voices told you that you would
be delivered in three months time?" That question
brought to the inspired girl's lips a prophecy that was
remarkable among all others by its mysterious form.
She answered that, in three months time, she would
be delivered by a great victory. "Don't be concerned
for your martyr," the saints told her, "accept every-

thing that happens, you will finally arrive at the kingdom of Paradise." The poor prisoner interpreted the saints' promise maybe in the sense of a human deliverance. But, at the stake, surrounded by flames, she certainly understood the meaning of her final deliverance, for she cried out from her bed of fire: "My Voices were not mistaken!" The three months had passed. It was May 30, 1431.

Joan of Arc was too much the daughter of the Holy Spirit not to have been a prophetess as much by her acts as by her words at the very least. It suffices to have read her story to feel strongly that one is in the presence of a prefigurer. She is a woman, she is a virgin, she is twenty years old, and her name is synonymous with deliverance.

Deliverance of the kingdom of God, deliverance of God himself. Deliverance of men by the Blood of Christ, deliverance of Christ by Fire. When Jesus, in his second Agony, called out to Elijah to deliver him, it was the Blood of the Victim of the world invoking liberation by Fire. *Elias quasi ignis*. From the top of the centuries, Jesus called out to Joan of Arc from up on his Cross, and Joan of Arc, at the stake, responded in her dying voice, pronouncing the name of *Jesus* and also asking for *Water* which is the symbol of the Father from whom the "Kingdom must come" at the end of ends. Such were the last words one heard...

It belongs to no man, and probably no angel, to determine, before the hour, what mystery of suffering, propitiatory immolation, and Consolation for all men, the Maid prefigured. But certainly there was an indescribable gulf there that we must be content to apperceive from an immense distance, at the center of the world, like an umbilicus of light!

Chapter 8: The Thaumaturge

Will Joan of Arc never be canonized?[30] Ecclesiastical jurisprudence requires miracles during the life and after the death of saints. By the will of the English no relic of the Maid having subsisted and the heroine having been monstruously deprived of a sepulture, no miracle can be certified over her *invisible* tomb. As for certain prodigies fulfilled before her martyrdom, and the dispersion of her ashes, it appears that one stamp is missing for them to be valid, insofar as miracles go, in the eyes of canonists or doctors of the Sacred Congregation of Rites. They did not seem supernatural enough to them. They really wanted to concede the Beatification which implies however Sainthood, but they do not dare go any further, and her public cult is adjourned.

One might believe however that the accomplishment of a prophecy *by the prophet herself* is a very incontestable miracle. Simple reason would have it like that. Now that is what Joan of Arc did constantly, before everyone's eyes, with unsurpassable evidence, to the dismay of France's enemies and for the admiration of all the world. Assuredly, no one is qualified to judge the Church, but it is permitted, sometimes, to its most respectful children to be surprised at its slowness or at its prudence.

---

[30]canonized: Joan of Arc was beatified in 1909, and canonized in 1920 (five years after this book was first published, in French, in 1915).

Not to mention the child who died outside of baptism at Lagny-sur-Marne, whom Joan resuscitated on May 18, 1430, five days before the Compiègne catastrophe, so that there would be enough time to baptize it; not to insist on this fact that modern historians have doubtless considered insufficiently patriotic or too naively legendary, – one has difficulty understanding, on the other hand, the irrecusable multitude of testimonies of clairvoyance and extra-human prescience that altogether comprise the history of the Blessed One, but which are not enough to determine an overwhelming affirmation of Supernaturalness.

Joan of Arc never wanted anyone to believe she was capable of a miracle, and she certainly did not believe it herself. The greatest saints have had the privilege of that sublime incredulity. One can even say that their ignorance in that regard is the essential condition of their power as thaumaturges. Absent from their visible acts and transported by a superior Reality, they find it completely simple that the laws of nature correspond to their translation, surprised only by the astonishment of other human beings who ought to have, like them, the plenitude of the Holy Spirit.

At Poitiers, the good women brought their chaplets and other objects to Joan *to touch*. "Touch them yourselves, they will need it as well," she told them. When the inhabitants of Troyes opened their gates to her, certain suspicions remained in the mind of some: was Joan from God or from the Devil? One could not believe that she was a creature like others. The Cordelier negotiator of the reddition, the friar

Richard, was charged with calming that agitation. When the Maid crossed the threshold of that city, Richard welcomed her publicly with signs of the cross and aspersions of holy water. Joan, by that means, had to be exorcised *as much as necessary*. The Maid then said in her *Lorrainian* dialect: "Come forward boldly, I won't fly away." That good French woman's cheerfulness was not only a mark of her generous race, it was above all proof of her perfect candor as an inspired virgin and could have also served to hide the profound tears that risked to betray her, while recalling Jesus' divine Tears at the tomb of Lazarus, when he was about to resurrect him.

She knew, and she did not know, being, as she said, "a poor girl," believing herself capable, all the more, of obeying and suffering. She wanted what God wanted, nothing else, but with what powerfulness and what presentiments of sorrow! What hidden tears she must have had! She had with her an adorable child of fourteen years, Louis de Contes, who was attached to her person and who followed her sometimes everywhere she went. Poor page! He saw his gentle lady weeping oftentimes, when she was on her knees on the tiles, suffering for not being believed, when she stated that, apart from the spineless kindness of the king, she had enemies at court, then when it was so necessary that she had friends! Later, when one was forced to believe her, she suffered yet again for being feared, and it was the same enemies but more implacable.

It is true that she had the love of the people and the confidence of the soldiers at that time. "She was the most popular general," says her military historian. "For her part, no injustice, no word of rancor or anger. A kind word, a fully gay quip, was, for Joan of Arc, the way to cut short an incident where her interlocutor had made mistakes. One cannot say it too often: to the qualities of strategist and tactician, she joined the merits of the most indefatigable of knights and the gayest of witticists. There is nothing in the fiction of poets that might give the idea of a set of qualities as contradictory in appearance, as lofty, as brilliant, as capable of seducing the most illustrious minds as of leading masses of people who judge based on appearances, on spiritedness, on vigorousness."

"It is by the grace of God and the Maid," said the soldiers, "that one receives only light wounds while fighting next to her." Yes, she was certain that those brave fellows whom she commanded and whom she had turned into French soldiers would have followed her anywhere, but she knew also that they were her escort, to accompany her all the way to the threshold of the prison of ignorance that was to precede her punishment.

What did she not see, having permission to read in the mysterious book of the Lord and in men's consciousnesses? One can suppose anything from such marvelous beings. Just how far could her prescience go, and what miracles would God have refused her, if she had wanted to enact them? But it was a large enough miracle for her merely to accomplish her mission as liberator of the kingdom, by giving to the king of France a *fatherland*! And still she had that sublime generosity to accept that her work might be fulfilled by unworthy hands compared to her own. For she could "kick the English out of France" by herself, as she said, the Lord of battles being at her command. There must have been at the bottom of her heart an act of heroic renunciation that the Angels were spectators to and that, alone, might explain the sudden break in her miraculous career, unexpected event that the most attentive history sheds no light on.

Not tolerating, either, neither blasphemy nor debauchery, she had however adopted for herself, with apparent mischievousness, the most innocent of oaths: *"By my martin!"* she said, when she needed vigorously to emphasize an affirmation. It is certain that an oath cannot be the object of a gloss or an exegesis. But for so extraordinary an individual, nothing is to be looked down on.

The expression so often used by common people – *Martin-bâton* – must have been intended to evoke, from its origin, the stick of Saint Martin, the patron saint of France. The stick was a symbol of command and an auxiliary of discipline. The *Bourgeois of Paris* said that "when none of the Maid's people seized me, she struck by large blows with her stick." Later that stick became the symbol of supreme command, of marshalcy.

It is permissible then to suppose that Joan of Arc's apparent oath held a certain sense of mystery for her, something like the signification of a miraculous power that had been transmitted to her by Saint Martin, protector of the Gauls.

"By my martin! I will make them come out alive." she said, affirming that she was going to Orleans. "By my martin! they will be taken alright, don't you doubt it." "By my martin! I will take it tomorrow, and I will return to the city over the bridge," she says to those who do not believe she will take the fortress des Augustins. Same expression when she wants to affirm that she will lead the king to Reims; when she expresses her desire to see Paris up close; same expression when she betrays her regret: "By my martin! the place had been taken!" And even before the fatal day of Compiègne: "By my martin! we are enough; I will go to my good friends of Compiègne." That cry recurs continually under the quill of the chronicler Perceval de Cagny, ocular and auricular witness.

Quite persuaded that Joan of Arc's real greatness is unknown, I firmly believe that she had a thaumaturgical power as exceptional as her Mission, and that she made merely the least use of it, economizing in that way – for the time of *Tenebrae* and Famines – the Glory of God and her own glory!

Chapter 9: Her Friends

Altior fuit universo populo ab humero et sursum.[31]
"He appeared taller than everyone by a head." It is
Saul whom the Bible spoke about like that, in the first
book of *Kings*. That unfortunate elect of the tribe of
Benjamin was designated for perdition. A head that
stands above others is infallibly condemned in advance. Superior beings hardly have any friends. It's a
law of nature. How could Joan of Arc escape, she
who surpassed her contemporaries by so much that, at
the distance of several centuries, it is impossible not
to see it? She had few friends then and for a small
amount of time, almost all proving unfaithful to her.

It would seem monstrous to call him a friend,
that puny prince whom she had made a king and who
sacrificed her immediately afterwards. One has tried
to disculpate the ingratitude of that fleur-de-lys'd little runt. One has mentioned the so-called tears that
would have been shed on learning about the hateful
punishment inflicted on the heroine, whom he didn't
lift a finger to save. But who would have been audacious enough to speak of his *friendship*?

"That king," says Jules Quicherat, "was he not
keen, even to the utmost, on her who had done the un-
believable for him? To take it a step further, what
feelings did Charles VII have for the Maid; people
will be greatly surprised when I say that that cannot
be seen distinctly in the five volumes of text I have
published. While all evidence shows Joan living and

---

[31]*Altior... sursum*: Samuel 10:23.

breathing only for her king, loving him with that ardor seen only for religious things, it stands out in a single testimony that Charles VII, on discovering her weeping one day, paid her many compliments and invited her to take a rest, being unable to endure the trouble she was giving herself for him. But as that scene took place the day before the trip to Reims, at a moment when Joan was using everything in her power to undertake it for him, and when, on the contrary, he was looking for a thousand pretexts to get out of it, it follows that he could not cause any more grief to the Maid than to speak to her as he did. Apart from that outburst of equivocal commiseration, we have only, in order to read the king's heart, inductions that his conduct gives way to... His heart! he hid it from impressions, as his person from view, always having lacked the so precious gift of magnanimity. Never, while the Maid was alive, was he completely subjugated by her. He always kept an ear cocked to collect evil rumors, unfavorable phrases. He listened, he kept silent, letting things run their course."

Try as one may, Charles VII cannot be counted among Joan of Arc's worst enemies, and that's already a great deal.

Among those who can be called her friends, one must first cite the most illustrious, Dunois, the great Bastard of Orleans. The first interview between Joan of Arc and that already famous warrior was rather rude, but he must have appreciated that certain women do not require a number of days to take authority. She had just arrived in Orleans and immediately began her paradoxical existence as a chief military officer.

"Are you," she said, "the Bastard of Orleans?"

"Yes, Joan," he responded.

"Who advised you to have us come through Sologne? Why did we not come by way of Beauce, right through the middle of the great English strength? The victuals were made to enter without making them pass by the river."

"Excuse me," retorted Dunois, "but that was decided on by the council of captains, given the strength of the English in Beauce."

"The council of My Lord," she responded animatedly, "is better than yours and that of men; it is surer and wiser. You thought to deceive me, you deceived yourselves."

Later, she threatened to have his "head removed." But nothing alters Dunois' chivalresque dispositions, and Jean knows quite well that she can count on his devotion. "Immediately I had placed my hope in her," said the twenty-six-year-old a little later, bringing his testimony before the inquest for the Rehabilitation of the torture victim. One may judge for oneself the strength of that extraordinary being by her being able to subjugate, from day one, so firm and so valiant a heart! That great warrior had the rare merit of effacing himself before that child and referring to her as the only salvation for Orleans and for France. He qualified his divine actions: *Credit ipsam Johannam fuisse missam a Deo et actus ejus in bello fuisse potius divino adspiramine quam spiritu humano.*[32]

He had also the character to say this: "Before she came, eight hundred or a thousand of my soldiers could not stand up to two hundred Englishmen: after her arrival, on the contrary, four or five hundred of mine had got the better of almost all the English force." He had seen her patriotic transports, her inspired enthusiasm, and after the length of twenty-six years, totally cooled by age, totally weighed down by the glory of one hundred combats, reliving his memories of youth, he spoke of her in that magnificent language, quite worthy of him who, in the words of Jean Chartier, was, "one of the finest speakers ever in the French language."

"Before me," she said, one day, to the king: "When I am afflicted that one does not listen to me better when I say something on the part of God, I retire and pray to God, I complain to him,... and, my prayer fulfilled, I hear a voice that cries to me: 'Daughter of God, go! go! I will be by your side, go!' And when I hear that voice, I am so happy and would always want to listen to it." And Dunois adds, "What was most extraordinary is that on her repeating those phrases of her Voices, she fixed her eyes on heaven, in marvelous transport."

Unfortunately, Dunois was only a servant of the king of France, and he was not permitted to follow Joan to the end. More unfortunate still, the true king was Trémouille whose name alone is a blot of

---

[32]*Credit... humano*: Latin for "He believes that same Joan to have been sent by God and her deeds in war were more inspired by a divine, rather than a human, spirit."

blood and mud on the sublimest pages of history. By that villain's perverse will, and as a result of his ascendent over Charles VII, the Saint's first companions of war, those of Orleans and those of the Loire, d'Alençon, Richemont, Ambroise de Loré, Jean de Bueil, Raoul de Gaucourt, the marshal de Boussac, the marshal de Rais who became a monster,[33] the sire de Graville, great master of crossbowmen and the sire de Culan, admiral of France, like Dunois, – they systematically separated from her, some abandoning her with heavy heart, and others by their own volition, such as that friar Pasquerel, her chaplain, who had been witness to the victorious girl's prodigies and who distanced himself ignobly from the captive, at the very instant when she would have had most need of his ministry. With the exception of La Hire and of Poton de Saintrailles who tried in vain to free her, the dispersion of her friends was complete.

In the end, and for her admirable campaign in Oise, which must have cost her so dearly, Joan, deprived of the assistance of all the powerful men, forgotten by the king who owed her for his not ending up a vagabond and who allowed her to be decried by the riffraff of his entourage, but wishing, all the same, with a fistful of loyal men, to continue her work, – Joan of Arc, greater maybe at her decline than in her days of glory, had become like a leader of partisans whom the first betrayal must have overcome.

The Maid's best friend and the surest was the executioner who opened the door of heaven for her!

---

[33]marshal de Rais... monster: See J.-K. Huysmans' *Là-bas*, or Georges Bataille's *The Trial of Gilles de Rais*.

Chapter 10: Her Enemies

"Never have I put my faith in anyone."

Such was Joan of Arc's response to the assassin-bishop Pierre Cauchon, insufficiently reassured by her chains and iron cage, which he had the villainy to inflict on his victim, and wishing to persuade her expressly not to attempt any escape. Already in Compiègne, on May 23, 1430, the day of her capture as the result of a diabolical betrayal, she gave that proud response to the Burgundian churls who had placed their hands on her.

"Give yourself over to me, and put your faith in me," each of them cried.

"I have put my faith in someone other than you," she said, "and I will keep my word to him."

That fact is perhaps unique at that end of the Middle Ages. Joan refusing to "put her faith," preferring death. At that epoch, such an act had nothing dishonorable about it. It was the case for many an illustrious captain, before, during, and after that terrible fifteenth century. Among the kings of France who "put their faith," one can cite John, called the Good, at Poitiers, and François 1st at Pavia. There was a recollection of the battles of old wherein the strongest gave "the gift of life" to the vanquished, this latter "giving his faith" in exchange. Honorable transaction for the both of them.

But Joan of Arc did not see it like that. Her

Faith was not that of others, nor any other. She was infinitely above all that could be offered in exchange and had no earthly compassion for the equivalent. Joan of Arc's faith was as broad and deep as all the sky of France and enough to satisfy the honor of ten thousand knights.

How could that be understood by a world wherein the noblest were for sale like cattle, when a word of honor had become an alimentary commodity profitable only to traitors and faithless people? It is a miracle, and the greatest of all miracles, that the Maid had been possible, for one single day, in that old society, among the bearers of famous names, vilified remnants of a lapsed feudalism, of a spent nobility, ambitious for money, pleasures, or personal vengeance, flunkeys designated for future monarchies that would gather all a nation into a single hand.

Joan of Arc's most notable and worst enemy was Georges de La Trémouille. "He was as bad a man," said Quicherat, "as Louis La Trémouille, his grandson, was an accomplished hero. Greedy, conspiratorial, despotic, foresworn, he had the art of making a name and a fortune for himself by hedging between two parties. Hateful to the Duke of Burgundy, who was the benefactor of his house, he became the valet of the youngest son of Brittany in order to gain intimacy through him with Charles VII and to supplant him finally. Moreover, he always kept suspect relations with his brother and other relatives, all functionaries in the palace or in the armies of Philip the Good. When the English invaded the Orleanais, in 1428, one saw in France, with a very suspicious eye, that they had spared Sully, Georges de la Trémouille's seigneury. Holding many great offices whose titles he appeared to have disdained, that detestable individual concentrated in his hands the direction of all affairs. He had two reasons for pleasing the king: the one so as not to admit that princes of the blood should approach the government; the other to see to it that the English force was beaten by foreign intervention. Fundamentally, his sole desire was to perpetuate a state of affairs that he found to his advantage. Independently of his authority at court, Poitou was like a possession of his, by means of the partisans whom he kept on salary."

Murderer of his wife fleeced beforehand, and, in principle, murderer of all those who opposed him, pillager and monstrous misappropriator of public funds, possessor thereby of immense riches, he enjoyed the intangibility of an official usurer, and the miserable king nowise blind, but always as in need of money as of character, demeaned himself to point of granting that feal rogue letters of remission for the most terrible crimes, qualified protocolarily as "peccadillos," *even before they had been perpetrated.*

One understands that the advent of the Angelic One must have rubbed that servant of the devil excessively in the wrong way. Without declaring himself manifestly hostile, without compromising his ascendency over the king, he could not at first show that he was opposed to a mission that appeared entirely divine and that was, in the eyes of the less favorable, the supreme recourse, for better or for worse, for the monarchy at bay. He forced himself even, in the early days, to feign a moderate admiration for the heroine. But he hindered her as much as he could, directly by his counsels or in a concealed fashion through the intrigues of his creatures, and, soon after the coronation, he unmasked himself, pretending that she had completed her mission and that it was temerarious at least to hope for a happy conclusion to her marvelous successes.

Charles VII's conduct, after his coronation, has always been a sort of historic enigma, explicable only in that way. Instead of marching subsequently on a demoralized Paris, as Joan asked him to do; when it seems, in order to achieve the conquest of his realm, that it would have sufficed for the king to want it, one sees him, without known cause, without averred motive, temporizing, groping around, making use of a calculated inertia, letting the opportunity pass which he should have seized, and misconstruing heaven's favors to the point of doubting her who had brought them to him! What must Joan of Arc have endured on seeing the party of politics and the skeptics, personified in La Trémouille, gaining the upper hand on her! From then on, Charles VII went looking for success through clandestine maneuvers, by base intrigue, instead of claiming his rights in plain view of heaven and arms in hand, supported by God's envoy!...

When one follows Joan of Arc, when one sees her fail before Paris, because of La Trémouille; – before la Charité and before Soissons, because of La Trémouille; before Compiègne, because of La Trémouille, without intervention of the authority of the king of France or the executioner's axe even;... then the tears of a compassion, as well as of a supernatural fear, burst out, as if one were witnessing the death of the Redeemer for a second time!

After La Trémouille, the first place among traitors belongs to Regnauld de Chartres, archbishop of Reims and chancellor of France. That man there is enough to discourage contempt. La Trémouille, at least, has this in his favor that he is a sumptuous rogue. Regnauld de Chartres, his principal instrument of iniquity, is nothing more than an envious skeptic and a bad priest, capable only of all timid infamies that the surprising baseness of his heart could suggest to him. When a job was unsavory enough to disgust even La Trémouille, he took charge of it voluntarily. That sinister individual brings to mind that archbishop of modern Paris canceling Joan of Arc's feast day celebrations because a king of England had just died!!!

Too inferior in intelligence and too little audacious to assume the role of a Cauchon,[34] he knew how to prepare the way for that judge and studiously maneuvered it so that in the end the heroine would be deprived of all human hope. Even then when the iniquitous judgment of a Saint condemned in advance had been worked out, Regnauld de Chartres, metropolitan archbishop, still could have saved the captive by demanding her from his suffragan in Beauvais who would have been forced to obey, given the ecclesiastical trial of Joan, monopolized by Cauchon, fell under his superior tribunal's jurisdiction.

---

[34]Cauchon: Pierre Cauchon (1371-1442), archbishop of Beauvais, responsible for having arranged Joan of Arc's trial.

Infinitely far from such an act of rudimentary equity, that prince of the Church domesticated by La Trémouille had for a long time worked to ruin Joan's trial. Before the catastrophe that was about to disarm France and prolong the war for another ten years, traveling to the surrounding areas of Lagny, Beauvais, Compiègne, Soissons, he revisited before the French captains the enormous damage, the incredible discredit that Joan's actions had caused all men of the sword. He proved to them that her victories, creating for her an ever-growing power, compared to the power of the ministers, was a veritable dictatorship that she would soon be exercising, with the unanimous enthusiasm of the people and the bourgeois. What would become of men of arms, once peace was imposed on the Burgundians and the English by the victorious Joan? Her dictatorship would be exercised under Charles VII's cover. It was not difficult to predict. With her pretension of moralizing the army, of chasing away the ribald from her ranks, of demanding from each soldier and captain respect for life and honor of others, it was a veritable revolution. The people and the bourgeois would gain all the benefits; as for the captains, they would pay for it. Goodbye privileges! Goodby immunities!

Such had been the apostolate of that successor of Saint Remi. Such had been the feelings and the practices of that servant of God, at the moment when Joan of Arc led that heroic campaign to the banks of the Oise; at the moment when she was delivering French populations from the terrible band of Franquet d'Arras; at the moment when the marvelous girl was organizing the amazing operation of Pont-l'Évêque, when everything was concerted to make the Duke of Burgundy's last army lay down their arms!

But that is nothing compared to the unprecedented letter of impudence and nastiness that he wrote, soon after Joan was taken, to the bourgeois of Reims supposed capable of taking it upon themselves spontaneously to free their heroine, – which would have been immensely disagreeable to La Trémouille and himself. "The object of the chancellor," said Quicherat, "is to announce to the people of Reims Joan's capture before Compiègne, but in such a way that their mourning is minimal." At first, he reports the fact briefly, dryly, then he immediately attacks the victim: "She did not want to believe counsel, and did whatever she pleased." The loss of such a haughty woman, is it really something to regret? "God has suffered the taking of the Maid because she had pumped herself up in pride and because she had done her will, not God's will." It was the stake already.

One is stunned to think that the author of that homicidal letter was a priest, a prince among priests! that he had seen Joan at Chinon; that he had been, at Poitiers, one of the doctors who, after having interrogated her, confirmed her as sent by God; that, four months later, having been a witness to her miracles, he had, by his own hands, crowned Charles VII in the cathedral of Reims, in the presence of that heroine who, hovering above the uncrossable chaos, came, by divine virtue, to effect the transfer of the old blood of kings on the throne of Saint Louis and Charlemagne!

Courage is needed to speak of Joan of Arc's other enemies. It is a filthy swarm. Nothing can compare to the sadness and disgust that submerges the heart on sight of that sublime character, one of the loftiest among those "whom the world is not worthy of," struggling in all her glory with reptiles and the stinking insects of the Abyss!

Long before Cauchon appeared and his contingents of doctors whose infamy terrifies; without going into the ignoble instruments used by the two aforementioned powerful villains, there were, to thwart her and to torture her on a daily basis, harmful and lamentable blind followers like Robert Le Maçon, "wise and faithful councillor under La Trémouille's discipline." Quicherat, who must always be consulted, judges him like this: "He was a hard-working man, entrenched in the practice of affairs that he understood marvelously, exempt from bad passions and those who spend their life amidst intrigues without ever suspecting them. The danger of such men is that their opinion, very considerable in matters within their sphere of knowledge, is reputed of equal value in other matters where there is only an echo of the former." It is known that one can make excellent executioners of innocent people from that sort of man.

Unfortunately one cannot exclude Raoul de Gaucourt from the cruel pack of Joan of Arc's enemies; he was one of the most energetic captains of that epoch, celebrated for his excellent defense of Harfleur against Henry V, in 1415, but an "old soldier little favorable to the glory of newcomers." Having served under Clisson and Sancerre, having fought against the Turks at Nicopolis, and all the civil wars in France, he was not disposed to admit that a girl from the fields could teach him a thing or two. A great danger that put him in opposition to Joan must have embittered him even more; because, while wishing to prevent a sortie commanded by her at Orleans, he nearly got himself massacred by the people. Rather than suffer such checks to his self-esteem, he preferred, he who was disquietude itself, to become the apostle of peace. After the coronation, he went, *on the part of the king*! to bear humiliating propositions to the Duke of Burgundy whom Joan wanted to fight... He corrected himself when it was too late, placed himself at the head of a coalition that toppled La Trémouille, and, the only surviving minister who had consummated the abandonment of the Maid, came to deliver his eulogy of her, in 1456, during the trial of rehabilitation, when he was 85 years old.

An altogether different man is Guillaume de Flavy. Some historians, like Wallon and Quicherat himself, have tried to hold him innocent of the enormous crime of having voluntarily caused the seizure of Joan of Arc before the walls of Compiègne, by giving the order to close the gate of the city on her. But all evidence points precisely to that individual being a soul damned by La Trémouille and Regnauld de Chartres who had the greatest interest in making the Maid disappear, she whose definitive triumph would have been their certain fall. They had to get rid of her at all costs. Unable and not daring to assassinate her, they took recourse in betraying her in the heat of battle, and Flavy, who had made his name sinister by an interminable suite of crimes, was wholly on point for that office.

But absolutely indefensible ignominy belongs to Luxembourg, guardian of the Maid at his chateau de Beaurevoir and having become thus the veritable arbiter, not only of her freedom, but of her death or life. Jean de Luxembourg possessed one of the greatest names of the Middle Ages. The stock of Luxembourgs, as old as Charlemagne, stretched across the empire of the Occident as far as Bohemia and Hungary. It was everywhere united with sovereign houses. Six queens, one empress, four kings of Hungary and Bohemia, as many emperors, made that name renowned in the world. The cardinal Pierre de Luxembourg, Jean's uncle, died in 1387, honored with the title of *Blessed* by popular acclamation.

All that to finish with the vendition of Judas! After horrible haggling, the illustrious seigneur hands the Maid over to her mortal enemies, in exchange for ten thousand *livres*, royal tax, which would be the equivalent today of 400,000 francs.

It was England that paid. Iscariot's quittance was given to it, in the following century, by John Calvin's apostles.

Chapter 11: The Tears

There is nothing but that. All is in vain, except the tears. History is like a dream because it is built on time which is an illusion, often dolorous and always ungraspable, but certainly an illusion that is impossible to fix. Each of the infinitesimal parcels, the whole of which constitutes what we call duration, rushes headlong into the gulf of the past with the speed of light, and history is nothing more than that swarming of glimmers recorded in the pupils of tortoises.

As history progresses, it soon becomes the secret of God, and even the greatest authenticity, in the eyes of the thinker, is but a *probable* opinion. However informed a historian might be, the fact he has before him, having so painfully collected it, like a ship wreck, from the bottom of the sea, he knows quite well that *he does not see it*. Its essential form, divine, escapes him necessarily. One has certain proofs, indisputable, of a large number of historic events at well-determined moments in time; but those proofs, fundamentally, have no other consistency than the absolute *necessity* of those events and times. That was what was NEEDED, and nothing else. Unique criterium.

Joan of Arc could have been freed or bought back by the king, – her death was not a necessary consequence of her captivity, as has been said. Without a doubt, but the opposite occurred, because those enormous injustices were indispensable to the realization of an enormously mysterious plan that we cannot be privy to.

Here are some strong lines by the captain Paul Marin whom I do not tire citing:

"History such as men write it! how to qualify it? It's a sketch of the truth, at the expense of the history – such as our minds conceive of – that God will read aloud on the last day, when the book unfolds, illustrating, in shafts of fire, billions of animated images, photographed at each minute that humanity has lived; an impartial book wherein each of the voices personifying billions of actors of passed dramas will repeat, word for word, the phrases of yesterday; a book whose mechanism defies the childishness of speakers and microphones! That great book of history, the day it is opened, will permit to judge, to compare, to place Joan of Arc on her level. After that appearance, the history written by historians... what will it be? Alas! less than a smoldering torch in comparison to the waves of light that the sun emits, when it emerges radiant from its Orient."

Then, once again, there is nothing but tears, when one is so loved by God to have them: *Beati qui lugent*. Tears, to be honest, cloud the view already so uncertain, but clairvoyance of the heart can replace it with an advantage, and a magnificent divination can illuminate the poor historian. And then, at a certain depth determined by the deposit of the illustrious dead, one is really forced to encounter universal Solidarity which is concealed to us by the social lie, and which their dust denounces with so much eloquence! That, above all, is what makes one weep!

One feels oneself to be on an equal footing in that excessive misery of all men. The dazzling effect of Heroism or Beauty has disappeared. Whether it has to do with Charlemagne, Napoleon, or Joan of Arc, one sees in them only one's neighbors or friends, very humble brothers in the immense herd of coheirs of the Explusion. Chants of glory, cries of enthusiasm, popular acclamations no longer exist; they never existed except in a dream that has evaporated. There is nothing left but tears of penitence, compassion, love, or despair, luminous or somber rivers that flow towards unknown gulfs.

Joan wept for pity over France, which the English devastated. In whatever place her soul resides, does she not weep still with a greater compassion over the same France immolated by even fiercer barbarians?

In 1846, there were the prophetic Tears of the Mother of Sorrows who wept on her Mountain,[35] supplicating her people to have pity for themselves, and those saintly Tears, which ought to be so criminally disdained, cannot fall to earth. Witnesses have told how they mounted towards heaven. What one needs today then are the tears of many millions of mothers or widows to replace them, and it is probably all that will remain of our contemporary history that already appears to be the most frightening of dreams!

---

[35]Mother of Sorrows... Mountain: Our Lady of La Salette.

Chapter 12: "Bishop, I die because of you!"

When speaking about Joan of Arc's judges, and in order to delay a little that revolting task still, it appears expedient to mention the rather little-known fact that follows.

After the iniquitous sentence of *relapse* that handed the saint over to the secular executioner succeeding the ecclesiastical executioners, and until the last minute of the last hour, it was possible to save her.

There existed in Rouen an ancient custom, royal privilege in ecclesiastical hands, "truly admirable and one of a kind and which, for that reason, merits being recognized by all, particularly in this France..." said the historian Pasquier. "I can say, whether one believes it or not, that in all antiquity, you will never find anything like it." That was the celebrated privilege of Saint Romain whom the English, able politicians that they are, had declared they "wanted to maintain and defend in honor and reverence of the glorious patron of the city," privilege that the people held in singular devotion and that had lasted until the end of the eighteenth century, in spite of the rights of royal power and the heightened sensibilities of judiciary bodies.

In virtue of that privilege of the *reliquary*, the cathedral chapter declared, each year, at the Feast of the Ascension, one prisoner free and absolved in a ceremony at which all the city's clergy took part, escorting with great pomp the reliquary of Saint Romain "raised" by the prisoner whom the Church had restored to both life and liberty.

In 1431, the Ascension fell on May 10. What would the English have done if the chapter had chosen Joan? And what would the people of Rouen have done if the English government had refused the chapter's choice of Joan? Prior refusals had caused bloodshed in the city. But the chapter lacked courage and, that year, by a truly bitter irony, instead of that innocent virgin the clergy designated a common prisoner, *guilty of rape*! The comparison with Barabbas stands out here glaringly.

The general cowardice decided by English ferocity with regards to the Maid is one of the most remarkable characteristics of the history of France in the fifteenth century. There are very few examples of such a failure of all men's courage. Joan was destined to be a necessary holocaust! And how greatly must God have wanted that height of iniquity which provoked his justice for the punishment of England, while at the same time it procured the greatest glory for its victim! The execrable Hundred Years War which was about to end was a terrible reckoning, and Joan of Arc's martyrization exceeded all measure.

We know the miserable end of her most tenacious judges and that of some of the powerful men whose servants they had been, dressed in infamy. We will come back to them. But divine justice demanded the head and entrails of England, just as it will demand the head and entrails of the German Empire. Henry VI, legitimate king of England on the death of Henry V his father, and so-called king of France by the death of his grandfather Charles VI, was not even ten years old when Bedford his uncle and the cardinal of Winchester his great uncle, veritable authors of Joan of Arc's condemnation, conducted him to Rouen so that that child might preside nominatively over the abominable trial, having decided, in the hopes of gaining him the kingdom, to engage him personally in their crime.

Now, here is the sentence that, without knowing it, the prevaricating judges pronounced. Henry VI would not lose merely the kingdom of France. The two crowns that had been placed on him in his cradle, neither of them, at the time of his death, belonged to him. After forty years of a dreadful civil war, the *White Rose*[36] would triumph finally, and that sad monarch, the plaything and instrument of factions for so long a time, would die at fifty years of age in the Tower of London, Gloucester's prisoner and victim, famous example of the malediction that strikes royal families after great crimes.

As for the English nation, it would need to expire hideously of apostasy in less than a century. The Tudor theologian and ribald would be born soon enough, and he would avenge Joan of Arc in his way, prostituting his people to a golden, arid cow. That would not cause anyone to blink an eye, *ad nutum regis*, and without martyrs nearly, for how many cen-

---

[36]White Rose: the House of York, in reference to the English War of the Roses.

turies? Overnight, all the kingdom that was, formerly, the Isle of Saints, would become heretical by the effect of an ignoble obedience...

"I know that the English will all be driven out of France," Joan had said to her judges, "all, except those who die here. I know this by revelation as clearly as I see you... Write it down, so that when it will have come to pass, one might remember that I said it." *Out of France!* Twelve years later, after the Battle of Castillon, and the death of old Talbot, that prediction was visibly fulfilled. But, coming from the mouth of Joan, who was so unjustly and so cruelly condemned, could such a threat signify less than expulsion from the Kingdom of Jesus Christ, a spiritual expulsion, an expulsion of souls, in the widest sense!

One is, or one could be, led to believe that Joan of Arc's trial, so ignored by the multitude and known only through some famous responses uttered by that heroine, is soiled with monstrous fraud and irregularities. Nothing of the sort. The minutes of judgment have been conserved, and it appears that it is one entirely irreproachable piece. "Drafted under Cauchon's lofty direction," wrote one eminent magistrate, "that work does honor to his English patriotism, to his juridical knowledge, and to his literary talents. It is difficult to find another trial so revolting at base and so ably concealed under hypocritical exteriors. Apparent respect for forms, scrupulous observation of the rights of defense (rendered illusory, in fact, by the obstinate refusal of any defense), nothing is lacking. But what good are forms when there is no spirit? Imagine today an entire judiciary personnel in cahoots to crush innocence: a public prosecutor, a judge of instruction, a chamber of accusation, a general prosecutor, a court of assizes, a jury. Innocence could be condemned within the rules. It is the case with Joan of Arc. When the register that contained the minutes of authentic instrument had been completed, it was then necessary to make copies or exemplified copies. Cauchon could have asked for only one, as is the case with so many trials. And then that lost exemplified copy, that trial, Joan of Arc's great glory could have disappeared forever. It did not happen like that, and it was the bishop himself, strange circumstance, who took the necessary precautions to immortalize his own infamy and the glory of his victim. The clerks of the court received the order from him to draw up five exemplified copies."

It would be a mistake to believe that Cauchon was any old mitre. Pierre Cauchon, "reverend father in Christ, by divine misericord, bishop of Beauvais," was, on the contrary, one of the most celebrated doctors of the church of his day, licensed in canon law, master es arts, doctor in theology, old rector of the University of Paris, and curator of its privileges; grand practitioner in matters of law, which the trial that has doomed his name to ignominy would suffice to establish, and one of the most engaged universitarians in the antinational cause. Promoted to the episcopate by the Burgundian faction in recompense for his zeal to launch a justification for the crime committed by John the Fearless at the council of Constance, excommunicated at Basel, anathematized later by the court of Rome, suspected of heresy and notoriously rebellious to the authority of the Holy See; – where

could the England of Lancaster and the *Red Rose*, future apostate and already anticipated, find a more de-
sirable servant?

Joan of Arc was doomed to a certain death on
the day when Bedford and the English cardinal had
decided to hand her over to Cauchon. What followed
was a matter of form and timing. To take up the hy-
pothesis put forward earlier, by which one imagines a
capital trial wherein each member of the jury would
have the absolute certainty of seeing all his property
confiscated and of his being skinned alive, in the case
of a verdict favorable to the accused or only invocato-
ry of attenuating circumstance, – one will have, in all
its exactitude, the situation of the judges or deliberat-
ing assessors, more than sixty of them, by whom Joan
had to be condemned. Cauchon was the best man in
the world to lead his flock in that direction.

It is undoubted that all those who condemned
Joan of Arc or who let her be condemned were absolutely sure of her innocence and that they all bore, to
their dying day, the shame and remorse of having par-
ticipated in that abuse of authority. One hundred ulte-
rior testimonies have demonstrated it superabundant-
ly. That unanimity of baseness or of cowardice is one
kind of prodigy that disconcerts. One has difficulty
imagining that multitude of priests, each of them cele-
brating, every day, the Holy Mysteries – one supposes
it at least – and, their mouths full of the Blood of
Christ, all the while consenting by deliberate resolu-
tion, *sciens et prudens*, to carry, for three months, the
enormous burden of that appalling complicity!

The majority of them knew, assuredly, what it

was that Joan called the *Book of Poitiers*, asked for by her so many times during the course of her interrogations, that is to say, the register of the first inquest which was so favorable to her at Poitiers and whose appearance at Rouen would have so fully justified her! That document must have been criminally destroyed at the instigation of Regnauld de Chartres.

Some, tortured clearly by their conscience, joined to their indictment that timid reserve that betrayed their anguish, while aggravating their injustice: "*Unless* the revelations of that girl did not come from God, *which is not presumable*." Others who were afraid, a prey to the vertigo of prevarication, grew enraged, like that canon of Rouen who had crushed the saint and who, a witness to her punishment, several days later, said this while weeping: "May it please God that my soul might go where her soul now is!"

Among those doctors and masters "having only God before their eyes and the truth of the faith," it would be unjust, in this case, not to make special mention of Guillaume Évrard, Burgundian theologian and vaunted preacher who, having been chosen by the bishop for a sermon wherein he had to anathematize Joan, carried his zeal of cowardice to the point of feigning against her, in his discourse, the most generous indignation. He also must have shed tears before her burning at the stake. The crocodiles all wept, it is said, and Cauchon himself did too, according to a witness.

Two only, already convoked and in the clutches of the demon of Beauvais, refused to take part in the trial. The first, Nicolas de Houppeville, aged theologian of 65 years, preferred to be thrown into prison without judgment on Cauchon's order, who did exactly whatever he wished. The second, master Jean Lohier, had the rare fortune of being able to escape, the same Cauchon wanting to have him thrown into the river. The testimony of the court clerk Manchon on the topic of that individual, twenty years later, sheds a singular light on that dark drama:

"Said master Jean Lohier, when he had seen the trial, – what had already been written – he said that it was not valid for several reasons. Firstly, because the trial followed no ordinary procedure. *Item*, because it was held behind closed doors where the assistants were not at full and pure liberty to speak according to their full and pure will. *Item*, because in said matter it treated of the honor of the King of France whom it represented, without appealing to the King or anyone who stood in for him. *Item*, because no court instruments had been drawn up or given and so that said woman had no council, who was a simple girl, to respond to so many masters and doctors of law, and in matters of great interest, and in especial those that touched on her revelations, as she said. And for all that it seemed to him the trial was not valid. Of which things monseigneur de Beauvais was extremely indignant against the said Lohier and said to the masters: 'There's Lohier who wants to give us some pretty interlocutories during our trial. He wants to calumniate everything and says that it is not valid. One can see clearly on which foot he stands!...' On the following day, I spoke to the said Lohier and asked him what he thought of the said trial and of the said Joan. He responded to me: 'You see the manner in which they proceed. They will catch her, if they can, by her words. It seems that they proceed more out of hatred than anything, and for that reason, I no longer wish to be here.'"

But not everyone could escape, and everyone shivered in his boots, except those who had condemned Joan before she was taken and who, holding her in their hands, ambitioned to burn her at the stake in order to please the English, and that alone could satisfy, and obtain from them, by that means, enormous recompenses.

The one who trembled the most, it was precisely the indispensable man without whom Cauchon could have done nothing, Jean Lemaître, deputy inquisitor at the trial. For a long time, he refused to take part, but it was made abundantly clear to him that if he continued to act thusly, he ran the risk of an early death. He made his decision only under pressure by the English, and one sees him constantly a prey to an extreme terror. "I see clearly," said the poor man, "that it will be my life if I do not submit to their will."

Beyond that, and without insisting any longer on the cowards or the ambitious of greater or lesser importance, the bishop of Beauvais had at his beck and call some very precious rogues and inestimable sacerdotal scoundrels. History has preserved the name of milord Jean d'Estivet, canon of the churches of Bayeux and Beauvais, appointed instigator or general prosecutor for the case, by reason of his "loyalty, probity, knowledge, sufficiency, and the suitableness of his venerable and discreet person," author of that draft or indictment, appalling by its imposture and hypocrisy, which sentenced the heroine to death. We are ignorant as to what could have been that admirable villain's ambition. Perhaps he did evil for evil's sake. Whatever the case might be, one knows that he got what he deserved. Several days after the burning at the stake, he was found dead at one of the gates of Rouen, drowned in a mud puddle.

There was also Loyseleur, the spy-priest abusing the sacrament of penance in order to betray Joan in prison, where the bishop had habilely concealed his listeners. That abominable individual, fleeing from the scene of the crime like a damned soul, scrammed to Basel where he died of a violent fit of apoplexy.

The others who turn one's stomach, even after the former, received their analogous salaries, and preserving their memory is not worth the ink used to write their names with.

The old University of Paris, venerated throughout the world, did not miss such a beautiful occasion to dishonor itself for time immemorial. That university, entirely English in sentiment, had made a gift to Cauchon of a half-dozen of its most illustrious doctors. They were, it appears, the most dogged and wily. Imagine for yourself the situation of a simple country girl, ignorant as far as can be of judicial forms and procedures, and the captious little schemes of theology, in the presence of that pack of heinous and perfidious scholars, her being deprived of counsel and forced to defend, one against all, her limpid soul!

She could remind herself of the evangelical warning: "Do not premeditate your responses. I myself will give you a voice and a wisdom that all your enemies will be unable to resist and contradict."

"Very sweet God," she said, "in honor of your holy Passion, I ask, if you love me, that you reveal to me how I must respond to these men of the church." One is familiar with her admirable and candid responses that constrained the pious and learned synagogue to dishonor themselves shamelessly, appallingly before posterity... "Joan," a witness said, "would have been unable to defend herself as she did, in so difficult a case, against so many and so great doctors, if she had not been inspirited."

And what rending compassion that must have been! Each interrogation lasted three, four hours and sometimes longer, advance punishment inflicted almost daily on a captive without a defender, extenuated by misery in a foul prison where, night and day, guards chosen from among the most horrible villains of the English army watched over her. That, by the formal will of the "Reverend Father in Christ" who hoped, doubtless, *charitably*, to wear her down by inanition and despair. It was even a question of subjecting her to torture, and they had the unqualifiable nastiness of placing before her the instruments of punishment, an abomination that horrified the executioner even. Opinions having been received, it was a matter of being resigned to them, one of the opining witnesses observing that there was no way that a trial "so well constructed" could expose itself to calumny.

"The assiduous work of your pastoral vigilance," wrote the University of Paris to Cauchon, "appears stimulated by the immense fervor of your very

singular charity; your tested wisdom will not cease to
be the strongest stay for the sacred faith; your experi-
ence, ever alert, comes to the aid of your pious desire
for public safety... We are anxious to give the greatest
thanks to Your Seigneury whose zeal does not rest for
one instant over the course of that important trial, un-
dertaken for the exaltation of the Divine Name, integrity, and glory of the orthodox faith and for the
most salutary edification of all faithful people...
Would that the Prince of pastors, when he stands before you, deign to accord you, for your revered solicitude, an undying crown of glory."!!!

Joan of Arc, the object of that solicitude, felt
lost. Her luminous innocence penetrated the heart of
that miserable judge on first appearance. It is to him
principally that her responses were directed, the others being in her pure eyes merely the terribly lamentable valets of her executioner:

"If you were well informed on my account,
you would wish me out of your hands... Pay close attention to what you say when you are my judge. I am
telling you, you take on a great responsibility by
charging me thus... I have been sent by God, I have
no business being here... You say that you are my
judge; I don't know that you are; but be careful you
don't judge me wrongly, for, in truth, I have been sent
by God, and you are putting yourself in grave danger;
and I am warning you, if Our Lord punishes you, I
have done my duty to tell you this. – I expect everything from God my creator. I expect everything from
my Judge. He is the king in heaven and on earth. – *I
often hear, through my Voices, news of you, mon-*

seigneur de Beauvais."

If one considers that Cauchon knew better than anyone the perfect innocence of her who spoke like that, one is forced, shuddering, to ask what His Seigneury's sleep was like after that, and what face he put on when he accepted his victim's last *adieu*, while he was escorting her to the stake: *"Bishop, I die because of you!* I appeal to you, before God!"

Moreover, for the entire length of that horrible trial of darkness and damnation, to suppose that the accursed man had a shred of conscience and a heart still capable of beating, if only in the manner of affectionate dogs, how could he not feel a small inkling of anguish on hearing the moaning of that Good Shepherd's sheep when her throat was cut in his presence and by his order:

"Do you want me to speak against myself? – Would you be content if I perjured myself? – Ah! you are good at writing whatever is against me, and you do not wish to write anything that is for me!"

That last complaint was made when Cauchon forbid the court clerks to register a declaration that could be seen as beneficial to her case. "Be quiet, *in the name of the devil!*" cried the pontiff to someone who attempted to intervene. He said it so loud that, despite the general fear, a long murmur ensued...

"I am waiting for Our Lord," she said with resignation when, after manipulating her words, they sought to make her contradict herself. There were some Englishmen in the audience who applauded her courage. "Truly, she is a brave woman! How English she seems!" exclaimed one of them.

The Reverend "Father in Christ" did not flinch when, as she no longer hoped for anything from this world, she asked for a Christian burial: "If my body dies in prison, I expect you to bury it in sacred ground. If you will not put it there, I will wait for my God to do it!" He knew quite well that the marvelous virgin's body would have no sepulture.

Joan of Arc, in effect, had that privilege of not having to submit to the corruption of the grave. Perhaps also there was no more sacred ground anymore in a kingdom where that appalling priest had set foot!

Chapter 13: The Holocaust

And Charles VII, King of France, Jesus Christ's Lieutenant, what was he doing? Absolutely nothing. He had his sojourn in Poitiers or Chinon, remaining nearly as much a stranger to the government as his father had been in the last period of his life and madness. La Trémouille and Regnauld de Chartres were they not there to govern in his stead? Charles continued not to see, to ignore the affairs of state, and not to reign at all. He probably knew nothing or very little touching on the case that was being debated in Rouen and to his evident prejudice, having nothing more to do with the moribund who had conserved his kingdom and whom he believed was no longer of use to him.

He could have, however, without risk and without fatigue, made at minimum a direct appeal either to the Pope or to the council at Basel, in convocation at that same moment. It would have been an immense help to Joan, from whom they went to great lengths to hide the fact that she could appeal to that great assembly as a last resort. The inquest at Poitiers, that Joan invoked so often in vain, had received sanction by the Inquisitor General of Toulouse, sanction by the clergy of Poitiers and, finally, sanction by Regnauld de Chartres himself, eminently qualified to introduce efficacious proceedings before the tribunal of Rouen. No instance of that kind was introduced. Joan had to die without a single clerk or lawyer presenting himself before the court in her defense.

No steps either had been taken by the king to obtain Joan's ransom. The sordid Luxembourg would have lent a hand voluntarily, for a price however, but how to gain the consent of La Trémouille, who held the royal purse strings and who untied them only for himself?

Finally and above all there was recourse to arms. La Hire was master of Louviers near Rouen, and the French occupied Beauvais and Compiègne. From those diverse points, the garrisons could have rapidly converged on upper Normandy. That nearness disquieted many of the English, "superstitious people," according to a common proverb, who did not dare begin a campaign again while the Maid was still alive. "The archives of La Rochelle, Tours, Orleans, Compiègne," said Charles VII's historian, Vallet de Viriville, "provide a number of testimonies by the people of those cities and those countrysides who had remained loyal, sympathetic, to her whom powerful men and fortune had betrayed. Charles VII, wouldn't he have had the army in his pay: those devoted cities would have delivered her to him. A single order by the king would have sufficed to set it in motion. The urban militia, what am I saying? the entire population that Joan had filled with enthusiasm, would have marched on Rouen for her deliverance, – men, woman and children, like the crusaders for the deliverance of the Holy Sepulcher."

But it was too much to ask of that idle king. Besides, he was leading up, from that period forward most probably, by diverse farces, to his famous role as the lover of Agnes Sorel, who must have earned him the very unheroic nickname of Charles the *Well Served*. That prince, whom God had extraordinarily graced by sending Joan of Arc to him, did not appear to have felt any remorse even for his monstruous ingratitude.

On November 10, 1449, Charles VII made his triumphant entry into the reconquered Norman capital. He stayed there for more than a week, amidst his entire court including Agnes Sorel, participating in the exaltation and drunkenness of the crowd. During that time, what did he do for Joan? Nothing. Not a thought for her whom the English themselves attributed their ruin to, for her whose martyrdom had made stones weep, having expiated, on that very site, the crime of having saved him! How to explain, at such a moment, that under the patriotic pressure of an entire emancipated people, Charles VII had not, at Rouen even, immediately struck that hateful judgment? Everything demanded it from him: the memory of the victim, the extent of service, his re-entry into that city where she had died for him, the outrage that her death caused to the entire country, and that unequalled hypocrisy that had sacrificed the saint to a hatred for the French! A prompt and brilliant action was needed... The best he could come up with was to stay silent, while caressing his Beautiful Lady who died, moreover, four months later, under rather mysterious circumstances.

It required the generous obstinacy of the cardinal of Estouteville, who felt the necessity of exonerating the Church of a crime one had wanted to heap on it, and the energetic will of Pope Callixtus III to obtain finally a revision to the trial and a sentence of rehabilitation proclaimed in 1456, twenty-five years after the abominable sentence.

The vilest thing in that poem of total and utter vileness is Joan of Arc's so-called abjuration. We know that there were, in reality, two trials: the trial of *lapse* and the trial of *relapse*.[37] The first, which had lasted for three months, was extended, and Joan was condemned. There was nothing left to do than burn her at the stake as a sorceress. But that was not a complete victory. It was necessary that Joan should retract her statements, that she should admit her Voices had tricked her, that she accuse herself, or that one might believe she had accused herself, of imposture, which would have had the effect of disqualifying her victories, invalidating the coronation, and dishonoring the king of France.

The heroine, in her normal state of mind, would have preferred death. They profited from a moment of extreme exhaustion, very calculated, to force her to sign a note of abjuration about which she understood absolutely nothing, other than perhaps that they would stop tormenting her then. At the inquest of 1456, many witnesses had deposed that at that very moment when they held her hand to sign, she was laughing like a madwoman!... "Considering," the sentence of rehabilitation said, "that the abjuration had been extorted by fraud and violence, in the presence of the executioner and under menace of fire, without the accused having understood the significance and

---

[37]lapse... relapse: in the sense of abandonment of the Catholic faith and/or having heretical beliefs.

the terms, etc..."

The grace it appeared that they were willing to grant her at that price was that same old loathsome and perpetual prison, "the bread of suffering and the water of anguish," as is said. Now, the English wanted to burn her at the stake. France needed to burn her at the stake in order to content those ferocious beasts, *crudelis et horrenda crematio.*[38] Cauchon knew this, but he was sure of being able to satisfy them, having predicted diabolically that Joan, after having come to her senses, would have invalidated energetically the cheap retraction wrested from her in her agony. To a lord, Warwick or Bedford, reproaching him wrathfully for having disappointed the English vengeance, he answered: "Not to worry, we will catch her soon enough": *Mox rehabebimus eam.*

In that famous and miserable trial, certain aspects of which seem particularly puerile to us today, one of the chief accusations against Joan of Arc was the men's clothing she wore, necessitated by her continual presence in the midst of soldiers and her refusal to take them off in prison where she was exposed, defenselessly, to the brutality of her guards. They were adamant that it was a crime against morality, a sacrilegious attack on divine law, on Holy Scripture, on Church canons. The putting on of women's clothing again was a consequence of the abjuration. She consented, believing that they were going to remove her to an ecclesiastical prison, where she would have also been exposed perhaps. They led her, instead, to the

---

[38]*crudelis... crematio*: Latin for "by cruel and horrendous cremation."

military roughs she had just quit and, the following
night, an English seigneur, a lord who remains name-
less, probable an accomplice of Cauchon the judge,
tried to rape her. She put on men's clothing again,
which were perfidiously left *within reach*. By this act
she was relapsed, all the more serious than when she
had made haste, formally, to disavow the abjuration.
Joy for Cauchon, who soon declared to Warwick and
to the people of his entourage: "*Farewell! Farewell!*
Make good cheer. This time, she is quite trapped."
The relapse trial was conducted instantaneously. Yes,
this time it was the stake without remission.

I spoke of tears earlier... How not to think
about Joan of Arc's tears? and how to think about
them as much as would be needed? Because she wept
with excessive bitterness, not only because of the
frightening punishment that awaited her, but principally, one can believe, on seeing, from her holy point
of view, all the human iniquity of which she was, ac-
cidentally, a victim, – her last tears having had to be
as mysterious as her destiny.

What a delight for France's enemies to make a
poor girl weep in that way, she who had frightened
them so greatly! The dazzling victress was reduced to
that, for those atrocious brutes, a poor girl who merit-
ed no pity. When friar Martin Ladvenu, sent by Cauchon, announced to her the hard and nasty death she
would suffer in several hours: "Alas!" she cried, "you
treat me like this, horribly and cruelly as can be, that
my body clean and whole, which has never been corrupted, should be consumed today and reduced to
ashes! Ha! Ha! I would rather be decapitated seven

times than to be burned like that. Alas! if only I was in the ecclesiastical prison that I had submitted to and where I would have been guarded by people of the Church, not by my enemies and adversaries, things would not have gone so miserably bad as they have! Oh! I appeal to God, the great Judge, for the great wrongs and violence that is done me!"

The end is unbearable. "She exited in women's clothing, and I led her then to the place of punishment," recounted the bailiff Massieu. "Along the way, she made such pitiable lamentations that my companion, friar Martin, and me, we could not hold back our tears. She entrusted her soul to God and to the saints so devoutly that all those who heard her wept." Nonetheless, before dying, she still had to endure a last and outrageous sermon by Master Nicolas Midi, one of her most frenetic judges. "In order to preserve the other members," that assassin said, "we are forced to cut off the rotten member. Joan, the Church, wishing to avoid infection, cuts you off from its body. It can no longer defend you. *Vade in pace!*" By the Church, naturally, he meant the clique of those damned Pharisees.

It is to be noted that the same Nicolas Midi, *having become leprous, not long after that sermon*, was called on, six years later, to harangue Charles VII, on his entry into Paris. The prostitution of those theologians and their audience, crowned or not, was enough to make one go mad.

At the end of the sermon, Joan prayed to all the priests who were there in large numbers, to say a mass for her, each one of them. But what mass could they say, if not the mass of virgin martyrs, and how was it possible for them to acquit themselves, with their hands covered in innocent blood, to hold the chalice, and with their fingers red with that blood, to bring the Body of Christ to their reprobative mouths?

My heart fails to go on. How to read, without trembling and weeping, that horrible page of the *Bourgeois de Paris*: "And soon she was, by all, sentenced to death and bound to a post that was on the scaffold made of plaster, and the fire under it; and then she fainted, and her dress was all burnt, and then the fire was behind her; and she was seen completely naked by all the people, and all the secrets that for a woman could be or should be kept secret, to remove any doubt in the people. And when they had seen enough, her all dead and bound to the post, the executioner stoked anew a great fire about that poor body that soon was all burnt, and the bones and flesh reduced to ashes. Many have said, there and elsewhere, that she was a martyr and on account of her just lord; others say no. So say the people; but whether it was bad or good that she did, she was burnt that day."

The incomparable general, the victor of armies, the taker of cities, Saint Joan of Arc ending like that! And the world needing more than four centuries to arrive at justice or compassion!

Conclusion

The Wooden Cross and the Iron Cross

When Joan of Arc was led to the stake, she asked for a cross to contemplate during her last moments. An Englishman made one out of two pieces of wood and presented it to her.

That Englishman, less vicious than others, who represented at that moment all of as-yet Catholic England, in spite of everything, would have been able to say to the martyr, as a priest addressing the people, on Good Friday, at the Adoration of the Cross: *Ecce Lignum Crucis*: "Behold the Cross where hangs the salvation of the world."

At that moment, the Maid understood what the Saints had announced to her of her deliverance and supreme victory, and she cried out, surrounded by the flames, that her Voices had not deceived her. That illuminative wooden cross fabricated by a compassionate rank-and-file soldier was the earthly recompense for her exploits and virtues. It sufficed for her to die.

The hateful and cruel roughneck who is the Emperor of heretical Germany offers today the iron Cross to his assassins and arsonists as recompense to them for their crimes, and he gives it to them as they stand before the inferno of cities set ablaze, their feet standing in the blood of populations whose neck they slit. That symbol of the Hohenzollern, that apostate iron cross is a sure prestige for exalting, insanely, the natural ferocity of his soldiers. Instead of world salvation, it is ruin and despair that are attached to that symbol from which darkness falls. And what a darkness!

It is the masterstroke by Luther, one hundred years after the Flower of the Middle Ages had been suffocated in the horrible flames of a burning at the stake, to have replaced the gentle wooden Cross which had consoled peoples and fortified Martyrs with that implacable iron cross that the world is terrified of. What the demons of the North have wanted to call German culture is, at four centuries of distance, the complete maturity, finally obtained, of the fruit of that accursed tree where the bad apostle was hanged. It is the definitive and supreme dissemination of Lutheranism.

Luther teaches, for example, that concubinary clerks *will be reformed* by making of their very disorder the general rule. Method of reform particularly suited to German genius, as Jacques Maritain, the already famous and victorious adversary of Bergson, has noted with deep insight, at his conferences on German philosophy.

"Does evil exist? We declare that it legitimate and necessary in and of itself. We will even place its first basis in God, as Jacob Bœhme did. Is this the German *me* with its natural instincts? We proclaim it, with Fichte, as the human type *par excellence*, before whom all must give way. Is this the war that will re-awaken forever, in effect, barbarous instincts? We will make barbarousness the rule of war even, which will be so much better the more barbarous it is."

In summary: "The revolt of Germany against Christianity, that's all there is to the Reform... that which was the discard and decay in Catholicism has become the norm and foundation in Protestantism and, through it, in the world and modern thought... The practice of hatred and cruelty regarded in itself as an office of religion, accomplished in the name of Christ and the Gospel. God with us, *Gott mit uns!*... Such is Luther's Germany, the Germany that we see at work today, for which to follow the instincts of covetousness, hatred, and lust is to be with God."

Such was the work of Luther, who found a Germany so well prepared to receive his doctrine that soon after the beginning of his *apostolate*, between 1525 and 1530, he could confirm for himself its effects. Here are the words of that patriarch of German culture: "Today, ours are seven times worse than they have ever been before. We steal, we lie, we deceive, we eat and drink to excess, and we abandon ourselves to all the vices... We other Germans, we have become the laughing stock and shame of all peoples; they take us for ignominious and obscene swine... If one wanted to paint Germany today, one would need to represent all the traits of a sow." And the same Luther whom one thinks one can hear speaking in 1915, from the bottom of his pit, deplores, without any sincerity however, "to have been born German, to have spoken and written in German, and he wishes to die in order not to witness the divine punishment that is ready to fall on Germany."

One could fill a volume with those testimonies by Luther who was never known to have repented them, but who hoped maybe to safeguard his memory in that way, all the while rejoicing like a demon over the appalling debasement he had been the artisan of. For a nation of brutes cultivated as brutes, it was a matter then uniquely of becoming the strongest nation materially and to merit the iron Cross which is the sign of material strength. It is against contemporary Germany that all other powers on earth must arm themselves.

The present horrors have an apocalyptic aspect that will become even clearer, one can foresee it. But the iron Cross will be vanquished in the end by the wooden Cross, because the latter is the choice of God and the sign of his preference. It could be, over the course of unimaginable events which the present war appears to be only the prelude to, that France in turn is condemned to a burning at the stake, like the Heroine by her apostate priests who repudiated the Mother of God while she wept on the Mountain of La Salette, while accusing them. Yes, France, always responsible for its spiritual leaders, could very well be condemned, by their criminal infidelity, to perish in horrible flames. All that would remain then is Joan of Arc's poor wooden Cross, which France does not want at this moment, but which would save it miraculously at the last hour so that humankind might not be lost.

The Cross of indigents and vagabonds, the

sweet Cross of old roads winding through the countryside, the welcoming Cross of the poverty-stricken, of the extremely downcast, their feet bleeding, their hearts tearful, those who have been bitten by serpents in the desert and who heal from their wounds while looking on the Cross of misery and glory!

– Bourg-la-Reine, February 6, 1915.

Appendix

Principle Works to Consult

SIMÉON LUCE. *Jeanne d'Arc à Domremy* (Critical research into the origins of the Mission of the Maid, accompanied by pieces of justification.) Paris, Champion, 1886.

The first part of this work appeared in 3 articles in the *Revue des Deux Mondes*: "Jeanne d'Arc et les Ordres mendiants" (May 1881); "Jeanne d'Arc et le culte du Mont Saint-Michel" (December 1882); "Jeanne d'Arc à Domremy" (May 1885).

QUICHERAT JULES, Director of the École des Chartes. *Procès de condamnation et de réhabilitation de Jeanne d'Arc*, published for the first time based on manuscripts from of the Bibliothèque, followed by all the historical documents. Société de l'histoire de France. Paris, Jules Renouard, 1841 to 1849. 5 vol. in-8.

Aperçus nouveaux sur l'histoire de Jeanne d'Arc. Paris, Renouard, 1850.

VALLET DE VIRIVILLE. *Histoire de Charles VII, roi de France, et de son époque (1403-1461)*. 3 vol. in-8. Paris, Renouard, 1863-1865.

O'REILLY. *Les deux procès de condamnation, les enquêtes et la sentence de réhabilitation de Jeanne d'Arc*, 2 vol. in-8. Paris, Plon, 1868.

HENRI CHAPOY. Les Compagnons de Jeanne d'Arc. Domremy-Reims (1412-1429). Paris, Bloud et Barral, 1897.

STEENACKERS. *Agnès Sorel et Charles VII*. Paris, Didier, 1868.

H. WALLON. *Jeanne d'Arc*. Paris, Dido, 1876.

PAUL MARIN. *Jeanne Darc* [sic]*, tacticien et stratégiste*, 2 vol. Paris, Baudoin, 1889-1890.

GÉNÉRAL FRÉDÉRIC CANONGE. *Jeanne d'Arc guerrière*. Paris, Nouvelle Librarie nationale, 1907.

ANDREW LANG. *La Pucelle de France*. Paris, Nelson.

ABBÉ CHASSAGNON. *Les Voix de Jeanne d'Arc*. Lyon, 1896.

ALBERT SARRAZIN. *Le bourreau de Jeanne d'Arc*. Rouen, 1910.

BOUCHER DE MOLANDON. *Mémoires de la Société archéologique et historique de l'Orléanais*. Orléans, Herluison, 1876.

Other Books by the Publisher

Fanchette's Pretty Little Foot
by Restif de La Bretonne

Je M'Accuse...
by Léon Bloy

My Hospitals & My Prisons
by Paul Verlaine

Salvation Through the Jews
by Léon Bloy

Words of a Demolitions Contractor
by Léon Bloy

Cellulely
by Paul Verlaine

Flowers of Bitumen
by Émile Goudeau

Songs for Her & Odes in Her Honor
by Paul Verlaine

On Huysmans' Tomb
by Léon Bloy

Ten Years a Bohemian
by Émile Goudeau

The Soul of Napoleon
by Léon Bloy

Other Books by the Publisher (cont.)

Blood of the Poor
by Léon Bloy

Theresa the Philosopher &
The Carmelite Extern Nun
by Marquis d'Argens &
Anne-Gabriel Meusnier de Querlon

A Platonic Love
by Paul Alexis

Two Novellas: Francine Cloarec's Funeral
and Benjamin Rozes
by Léon Hennique

The Revealer of the Globe: Christopher Columbus
& His Future Beatification (Part One)
by Léon Bloy